About the author

My name is Wynn Johnson. I was born June 28th, 1954, in the coal fields of south-east Kentucky. I left home at an early age in search of success and adventure. Formal education came to me in bits and pieces throughout my adult life. Courses, classes and credits amount to just over two years of college. However, the education I'm most proud of has been from the thousands of books I have read and the millions of miles I have traveled. I have learned that it would be next to impossible to get through life without at least the amount of education that I have achieved.

I made it a point to learn from my travel and there has not been a journey that I didn't learn from. There was always something to learn. A river, mountain or other natural or man-made landmark has always caught my attention. Bridges have always fascinated me. A covered bridge in western Indiana to the twenty-mile-long Chesapeake Bay bridge, or the bridge crossing the Grand Canyon near the Hoover Dam. But many things fascinate me and that has made it easy for me to learn.

My joy of reading has been such a blessing in helping me to become a writer. I don't go out of my way to use words that are not used in common conversation. Doing so makes reading more work than fun and most readers are not looking to expand their vocabulary. Therefore, I try to write in the same simple way in which I speak.

I still enjoy traveling. But when nature takes away my ability to do so, I will take my journeys with the pages of a book. That is the kind of books I look for. Those books that take me places with very little imagination. And that is the kind of author I try to be. To take you to places and show you things. To form pictures in your mind, to make you smell fragrances or feel the wind, the cold or the heat. And to use as few words as possible in doing so.

As I have promised my readers and as I have written in previous books, I must add this. There are two issues in the world today, that eliminated, would solve the problems of humanity. Those problems are hunger and illiteracy. I believe that the answer to any question, or the solution to any problem, can be found on the pages of a book. So, put down the phone, close the computer and open a book.

A SOJOURN LIFE

WYNN JOHNSON

A SOJOURN LIFE

Vanguard Press

A CIP catalogue record for this title is
available from the British Library.

ISBN 978 1 80016 327 0

*Vanguard Press is an imprint of
Pegasus Elliot MacKenzie Publishers Ltd.*
www.pegasuspublishers.com

First Published in 2022

**Vanguard Press
Sheraton House Castle Park
Cambridge England**

Printed & Bound in Great Britain

Acknowledgements

Writing a book is a lot of fun, but it's also a lot of work. No one who has ever written a book can say, with honesty, that they did it all by themselves. There are lots of people who play a part in producing books, and I hope I don't forget anyone. First, I want to thank everyone who read my previous books. It's hard to describe the elation, and the honor, I felt when the first person read my first book. I still feel the same with each new reader.

Once again, as before, the first person who read this book as a manuscript was Katy Newton Stein. Katy is an avid reader, and it meant so much to me to get her thumbs up.

There are also those who played a personal, and hands-on part in this book. I would like to thank Judith Palmateer, the publisher of my first book. I want to thank my sweetheart, and personal advisor, Jessica Stockwell. And once again, I want to thank Jamie Fischer, who has always been a help and a motivator. My sincere appreciation for my lovely granddaughter, Cassie Roberts, for her amazing photography skills in creating the photo for the book cover.

And a heartfelt thanks, to Suzanne Mulvey, Vicky Gorry, and all the fine folks at Pegasus.

Also by Wynn Johnson

An Angel is Born
(2013)

Lische
(2017)

Tales of the Moon
(2019)

Eldorado

Gaily bedight,
A gallant knight,
In sunshine and in shadow,
Had journeyed long,
Singing a song,
In search of Eldorado.

But he grew old-
This knight so bold-
And o'er his heart a shadow,
Fell as he found,
No spot of ground,
That looked like Eldorado.

And as his strength,
Failed him at length,
He met a pilgrim shadow-
"Shadow," said he,
"Where can it be-
This land of Eldorado?"

"Over the mountains Of the Moon, Down the Valley of
the Shadow,

Ride, boldly ride,"
The shade replied,
"If you seek for Eldorado!"

Edgar Allan Poe, 1849

Preface

Just before five a.m. on August 24th 1992, hurricane Andrew made landfall in south Florida near Elliott Key. The strongest wind gusts were recorded at 177 miles per hour and a barometric pressure of 922 millibar. This was the strongest wind gusts since hurricane Camille and the lowest barometric pressure to date. Those were the last readings before all instruments failed. The Air Force base at Homestead had been evacuated and the planes flown to safety. However, the damage to the base was so severe, it was never rebuilt.

The storm then blew across the Gulf of Mexico and made landfall again twenty miles south-west of Morgan City, Louisiana. With sustained winds of 115 miles per hour, the storm then turned north-east leaving death and destruction in its wake.

In south Florida, forty-two people had been killed. More than 600,000 homes and businesses were destroyed and 1.4 million were left without power, water, sewer, or communications. Many had escaped, but others wandered dazed and confused through the rubble.

I was living in Columbus, Ohio, working as a lineman for a large telecommunications contractor.

Utility companies in south Florida were asking for help in rebuilding and restoring service to the area. Just days after the hurricane, I was on my way to south Florida. I didn't know it then, but my life would never be the same.

Chapter One

As a marine I had traveled to a great number of places in the world. In fact, at that time, I had been to more countries than states. I was going to be going to places I had never seen. I had been to Atlanta, but only in a plane. I had a connecting flight which took me from there to Charleston, South Carolina, then a bus to Paris Island for boot camp. Beyond Knoxville it would all be new to me. I wasn't sure just how I felt about that. Although I had always looked for adventure, something about this trip was unnerving.

Those of us who had agreed to go, were given very little time to prepare. The need for help in south Florida after hurricane Andrew was urgent. I put my things in storage, I knew I would be gone for a long time. I loaded everything I needed into my work truck and left Columbus on August 29th 1992.

I would take interstate 71, from Columbus to Cincinnati, then south 75 all the way to Florida. I would stop for the night somewhere south of Atlanta and again just north of Fort Lauderdale. That would put me within thirty miles of the check-in site.

I have never liked endings or saying goodbye. When a day ends, we know we will never be able to live that day again. When we leave a place, we always wonder if we will ever see that place again. When we say goodbye to someone, we could be ending a relationship forever without ever seeing that person again. I guess that's why I felt so melancholy when I left Columbus.

It was just getting daylight when I got to Cincinnati. The city was just waking up and the traffic was light. I've always loved that city. It has its share of glimmering glass skyscrapers in the center of town. Many of the suburbs have their homes perched high on the hills and bluffs overlooking the Ohio River. A lot of people don't realize that nearly half of the city of Cincinnati is in Kentucky. In fact, the Cincinnati airport is in Florence, Kentucky, nearly twenty miles south of downtown.

Downtown Cincinnati is situated along the north side of the Ohio River. There is a mountain running parallel to the river on the south side and the city of Covington, Kentucky. The mountain is covered with houses, apartment and condominium buildings. I thought about the folks in those homes. Strolling out for the morning paper, making coffee, reading the paper, having breakfast and planning a normal day. Nothing normal about my day and I wondered if it would ever be normal again.

As I got to the top of the hill on interstate 75, I glanced in the rear-view mirror for one last look at downtown Cincinnati and Ohio River. Another half hour and I was completely out of town headed straight due south over the rolling hills of northern Kentucky. It was still August, but I had already noticed some yellow leaves. Probably not from autumn, but from the stress of the summer heat.

Northern Kentucky is a beautiful area. There were still a few tobacco fields, but most fields were now corn, soy beans, or horse pastures. If you've never been to Kentucky's horse country, it should be added to your travel list.

It was mid-morning; the sun was bright, and patches of mist was rising from the lowlands. Late summer flowers were blooming in gardens and along fences. In the meadows, nature had her collection of flowers. There were black-eyed susan , water lilies, daisies, wild parsnip, and of course, golden rod. There was also a flower that my mother called frost flowers. I never knew the official name for them, but they grow wild in pastures and meadows. They grow to a height of three to four feet in height, and the flower is a deep purple. Mother always said that when they bloom it's only six weeks until frost.

Even from the interstate I could see neatly painted and well-kept houses and barns. White wooden fences stretched along green pastures, yards and driveways. There was something peaceful about watching horses graze. It's as if they've never had, nor will they ever have, a care in the world.

I stopped at a rest stop about forty miles north of Lexington. A man in the restroom asked which direction I was going, and I said south. He asked if I would let him ride along. I asked where he was going, and he said, "Lexton." I knew in an instant he was drunk, but he looked harmless enough, so I said yes. However, I told him I had to be in south Florida by Monday morning and I would not go out of my way. I would take the first exit ramp for Lexington, drop him off and be on my way. I was thirty-eight years old then. He looked to be about my age, but he looked as if he had been through some tough times. Although probably self-inflicted. His clothes were dirty, and he smelled of sweat and liquor. His hair was light brown, thin on top, and it looked as if he had some teeth missing.

I moved some things from the floorboard on the passenger side to the back seat and told him to get in. After a long fit of hacking and coughing he said, "Nice truck."

I said, "Thanks. So where do you live?"

He only said, "Lexton."

I said, "What brings you so far from home?"

He said, "A woman in Cincinnati." He then proceeded to tell me what a lousy person she was. He said she had invited him to come and see her at a trailer park in the suburb of Sharonville. It took him nearly all night to get there, and when he knocked at the door, a man opened the door and kicked him. He kicked him just above the waist, a blow so hard, it knocked him backward over the railing. He said he was either knocked out or passed out on her lawn. When he woke up, he just started walking and hitch-hiking toward Lexington. He then proceeded to call her several bad names as his voice faded and he fell asleep.

He probably hadn't had anything to drink, but there was still a strong odor of alcohol from the night before. In less than an hour, I took the exit ramp for Lexington. I tapped him on the shoulder and told him he would have to get out. He looked around, looked confused, then coughed again. He said, "You know, I just live over in Versailles."

I said, "That's nice. I thought you lived in Lexington."

He said, "Versailles is just on the other side of Lexington."

I said, "Oh, I see. Well hop out and I'll be on my way."

He said, "Come on man. It's only about twenty minutes from here."

I said, "That's twenty minutes there and twenty minutes back. I can be fifty miles down the road in that amount of time."

He said, "It just don't make no sense to pick a man up along the road and put him right back out on the road again."

I said, "You're probably right. I should have left you at the rest stop."

He said, "Yeah, and that's why you're going to take me to Versailles."

I turned off the engine, removing the keys as I got out of the truck. As I rushed to the other side of the truck, he threw open the door and yelled, "What the hell is going on?" He put his right foot on the ground, and at that same instant, I had a firm hold on his right arm at the wrist and above the elbow. He turned to face me, placing his other foot on the ground. I braced myself and pulled with all my strength. He remained partially bent at the waist, taking long awkward steps as I swung him toward the tall weeds along the ramp. He landed face first, yelling obscenities. I got back into my truck and drove away.

A few miles down the road, the anger had left me, and I was breathing normally again. I didn't regret throwing the guy in the weeds, my regret was that I had ever met him. The whole thing just added to my melancholy state of mind. I turned on the radio and searched the channels for a classic rock station. Unsatisfied with that, I pushed in a cassette tape of Foreigner's *Agent Provocateur*, and turned the volume to blasting.

I had noticed some clouds along the south-west horizon. It had been an extremely hot and humid summer. The thought of a cooling shower was refreshing. For the next few miles, my view of the horizon was blocked by hills and trees, but the bright sunlight faded, and the day became dark and overcast. I passed a sign that read, 'Jellico Tennessee 15 miles'. Large raindrops began to fall as I started up the slopes of Jellico Mountain, the summit of which divided Kentucky and Tennessee. I came up behind a semi that was slowing down due to the grade. Rain was falling so hard now that visibility was reduced to a couple hundred yards. I positioned myself a safe distance from the back of the truck and was content to follow at a slower speed.

It was what everyone calls, 'a white knuckle drive'. The only thing I could see was the lights on the back of that truck. It seemed to take forever, but I was relieved to reach the summit, and a sign that read, 'Welcome to Tennessee, The Volunteer State'. A short distance beyond that a sign read, 'Scenic Overlook, Next Right'. I took the exit, pulled into the parking area and turned off the engine. Rain was still pouring, and the temperature outside had dropped dramatically. I opened the window a couple of inches, put the seat back and closed my eyes for a nap.

It was just a fast moving, late summer thunderstorm. I slept for almost an hour. I awakened to the sound of a very loud robin. The rain had stopped and there was a pale warm sun shining through the windshield. I got out, stretched, and walked to the overlook. About halfway down the mountain, mist was rising from the forest. Deep in the valley below, the city of Jellico looked like a tiny toy village.

The lonely feelings came back to me as I reflected on the day. I was suddenly feeling sorry for the man I threw into the weeds a couple hours ago. I wondered if I could have handled that situation differently. I wondered if the man would be all right. Then I began to look back over the past ten years. I had given up or thrown away a lot for this new beginning. Then I thought of the words of Walt Whitman, who said, "When the gods want to punish you, they listen to your prayers." But I felt I was on a one-way journey. I got into my truck and headed south.

Chapter Two

The rest of the trip was uneventful. I made my final stop at an Econo Lodge just north of Fort Lauderdale. The eastern horizon was just beginning to glow when I headed south toward Miami-Dade County the next morning. I stopped at a Walgreens and bought a map of Miami-Dade County. I drove west about seven miles, then turned south on what I thought would be a less traveled road. I was still about twenty miles to my destination, when I noticed, that all the trees that were left standing were pointed to the west. I thought I was still well out of the city until I passed the new Joe Robbie stadium. I soon realized, there were no less traveled roads near Miami.

It was not yet seven a.m. and I could already feel the heat of the sun on the truck window. In the military, I had served in the tropics. Therefore, I knew there was still a lot of summer left in south Florida. It was stop and go traffic going south, and the northbound lanes were bumper to bumper with convoys of large trucks loaded with rubble.

The company I was working for was National Communications, or Nacom. They had rented a large warehouse near the end of the westbound runway of

Miami International Airport. The noise was sometimes horrendous. There were lots of trucks and vans parked in front of the building, but I didn't see anyone. I saw a sign on the office door which read, 'Nacom, Crew meeting eight a.m.' I had almost an hour to kill, so I took out the western novel I was reading, put the seat back and relaxed. I was pretty sure it would be my last opportunity to do so.

We formed a circle in the warehouse and introduced ourselves. There were thirty-two of us and we were each given a tech number. This number was the code we would need to report repairs. Mine was 827. There would be no production until the following day. The first day would be spent stocking our trucks and getting settled in. We were issued two-way radios with a range of seventy miles. Those radios would prove to be the most important tool we could have ever hoped for.

The man in charge was a gentleman from the bay area of Virginia. His name was Glen Allen. He pointed to the north and said, "When you leave here, go to that red light and take a right. That road dead ends at Collins Avenue. Make a left on Collins and the Howard Johnsons hotel is about two or three blocks on the right. It's fifteen or twenty miles, but it can take hours to get there." We all laughed. We thought he was joking.

Glen had a map of the city tacked to a sheet of plywood with areas marked in various colors. He pointed to the board and said, "We are here, anything to the south is completely devastated. One of the first signs that you're entering the storm path is an interstate highway sign sticking out of the front of a building on your right. That sign says, 'Interstate 75'. I-75 is over ten miles to the east.

"Florida Power and Light crews are putting up the poles. We're going to be right behind them stringing three-eighth-inch steel strand cable. We will hang overhead drops to the few houses that are left standing. We will begin with the city of Kendal, work our way south and east toward Coral Gables, Florida City and Homestead. Many of these streets are still blocked, and there are no street signs. Do the best you can. You'll meet Pablo on your way out. He will issue magnetic signs for your vehicle." He held up one of the signs, it read, 'Supporting Bell South, Emergency Disaster Relief'. "These signs are to remain on your vehicles at all times, or they will be towed away. Be here at seven a.m., give yourself plenty of time."

Miami is in a perpetual state of rush hour, but add to that, the thousands who were brought in to help with storm damage. Military troops were brought in to prevent looting and help with traffic control. Every hotel and motel in the area was full. I left Nacom's building at about twelve forty-five p.m. I reached the east end of the Biscayne Bay bridge just after three p.m. entering the city of Miami Beach. Two hours and forty-five minutes to travel about twenty miles. There was a small bank on the right, I stopped to open an account and pick up a green machine card.

A few more blocks and I turned left onto Collins Avenue. I was agape at what I saw. For lack of better words, it was a concrete and glass canyon. Hotels and condominium buildings stretched skyward on both sides of the street. Collins Avenue runs from the southern tip of South Beach, running north through North Beach and crosses a bridge to the mainland and the city of Hollywood.

The Howard Johnson stood on a small hill. I pulled up to the stately manor where sharp-dressed valet personnel stood at the ready. They acted as if they were expecting me. They said they would be happy to park my truck, or I could park in a lot across the street that was reserved for us. They told me I could set out whatever I intended to take to my room and they would keep an eye on it until I came back. I set out my bags and asked about security for the parking lot, as I had some expensive electronic testing equipment in my truck. They said not to worry, they were on duty twenty-four hours a day, and the parking area was in plain view.

The hotel was an old but beautiful building. The walls of the lobby were covered with angelic murals and mirrors. There were large planters with tropical plants and flowers. At the rear of the lobby near the elevator bank, someone was playing softly on a piano.

I dragged my bags to the counter and a striking young lady said, with a Spanish accent, "Hello. My name is Isabella, I am your concierge. Would you like ocean view or bay view?"

I said, "Well, if I have a choice, I would love to have ocean view."

She said, "I have one left on the eighth floor."

I said, "That sounds perfect."

She said, "We have a restaurant and lounge downstairs, we also serve food and drinks outside at our tiki bar."

I freshened up a bit, then took the elevator to the bottom floor. I stepped out of the elevator into another elaborate setting. The restaurant had a tall ceiling and walls covered with mirrors. There were lots of tables and chairs all polished to a shine. In the center of it all was a large circular bar with three bartenders. I walked on through the place and outside where there was a long kidney-bean-shaped swimming pool. Beyond that was a circular tiki bar with a roof that was covered with coconut fronds. Beyond that was the boardwalk, the beach and the ocean.

There was a loud and boisterous group of men sitting around the bar whom I recognized as my co-workers. There was one voice that could be heard above all the noise. It was the voice of a huge sasquatch looking fellow by the name of Charles Beam. He stood about six foot four inches. He had long black curly hair and beard. He wore a Jack Daniels T-shirt that didn't quite cover his bulging stomach. The pretty young ladies behind the bar were Spanish speaking ladies who had not yet learned to speak English. However, they understood enough to cringe each time he yelled, "A whore, get me another beer."

I took a seat at the bar as far as I could get from him and ordered a Bud Light draft. The guys were talking among themselves, but I don't think anyone was paying attention to Charles Beam. I knew it would not be long before he tried to strike up a conversation with me. I heard him say earlier that he was from Louisville, Kentucky. Kentucky is my own home state, but I wanted no connection with him whatsoever. He asked in a low growling voice, "Where you from?"

I just said, "Ohio."

As I reached for my beer, he said, "Well, you know what they say about Ohio." I didn't respond. I just took my beer and my western novel and headed for the boardwalk.

To me, there's always been something mesmerizing about the sea. I sat there looking out at the blue/green beauty and the peacefulness of the Atlantic Ocean. It was hard to imagine, how just a few days before, that peaceful beauty was a killing fury.

The sun was going down behind me, the temperature and humidity had dropped. The sky in the east had turned to a slate blue. There was hardly anyone on the beach. Perhaps it was because it was Monday evening. Then I noticed a bright light, far out over the ocean. It resembled an extremely bright star. I realized it was an airliner headed for Miami International

Airport. Behind that plane was another, and another. I began to wonder where all those planes were coming from. Were those people on board coming home, or did they have connecting flights and headed for who knows where? There was, no doubt, happy people on those planes. But I'm sure there were sad ones as well. Folks coming from funerals, and folks going to funerals. I had been on the boardwalk for over an hour, and tomorrow would be a busy day. I dropped the empty mug at the tiki bar and headed for my room.

Chapter Three

I stopped by the front desk and asked for a four a.m. wake-up call, but I really didn't sleep that night. I'm not sure if I was excited about getting started or nervous. When I got out of the shower at four thirty a.m., I could already hear voices in the hall, and doors slamming. I guess everyone else was nervous as well. At twenty minutes to five, I headed out, but the traffic was already backed up before I got to the Biscayne Bay bridge. I made it to the warehouse just before seven a.m.

Pablo was the dispatcher. He was on the two-way radio calling each tech to get their ETA. We would wait until everyone arrived, then convoy into the work zone. I was in the parking lot speaking with two men from Minnesota. Rob Costell was from Fridley, Minnesota, and Ron Lenartson was from Cottage Grove, Minnesota. Lenartson was the quality control inspector. The three of us were discussing standards and techniques, when a man walked into our circle talking about the special sales available at K Mart. He rattled on and on about the great deal he just got on light bulbs. He said, "I was there when they opened, cause I wanted to get the good bulbs before they sold out, this is the good bulbs, cause they last twice as long. I'm going to replace all the bulbs in my house, even though I don't live in the house, it's got ghosts in it, two of 'em, the city sent me a bill for mowing the grass, but I told em I already paid it, so they sent me two more bills, I'll go back when my birthday comes in May, if those kids across the street don't make too much noise."

The man then turned and rushed away. I couldn't quite grasp what was happening. I said to Ron, "What was that man talking about? And since we're living in a hotel, why does he need light bulbs?"

Ron said, "Oh that's Jim Geovanni. I know him from Minneapolis. He's crazy as hell, but he'll work, and we need all the manpower we can get." I could see that there was going to be some interesting characters within this operation.

We were each issued a case of bottled water and advised not to share with the locals, due to the difficulty in getting supplies. There was a constant flow of trucks coming into the area, and a constant flow going out carrying brush and rubble. There was an unforgettable smell in the air. There was the smell of trees and vegetation drying in the tropical heat, but there was something else. We believed it to have been the left-over presence of death.

It only took about forty-five minutes to reach our starting point. The pole lines passed behind rows of houses. The power company had used heavy equipment to plow a path through the rubble. Homes in south Florida are built to withstand heavy storms. There are no basements. Houses are single story, slab on grade and walls both inside and out are built of cinder block then covered with plaster or stucco. However, no one had ever seen a storm of this magnitude. In most cases, the walls remained standing, but the roofs, windows, doors and anything that wasn't concrete was blown away.

I climbed the first pole, hooked my safety belt and looked out over the landscape. As far as I could see in every direction was houses with no roofs. Except for the fact that the ground was covered in rubble, the entire area looked as if it were under construction. As if roofing, doors and windows had not yet been installed. I thought all those people had been displaced, but by midday I realized there was life within the ruins of those homes. They would leave home in the morning and return about mid-afternoon. Some on foot and some in cars if they had one that hadn't been destroyed and the streets had been cleared. I also noticed that they picked up people along the way. They were not going to work, they were going to stand in the relief lines for food and water. When they returned, they searched through the rubble for personal items, such as small household items, clothing or photographs. But most of the things they found, had belonged to some distant neighbor.

I listened to the two-way radio chatter, to connect faces to names. Word came that work would stop at four p.m., until more poles were set, and more streets were cleared. The trip back to the hotel took well over three hours. I took a shower and went out to the tiki bar where I ordered a burger and a tap beer. The mood among the crew was completely different. I could tell everyone had been affected by what they had seen during the day. Charles Beam was even less obnoxious. I reintroduced myself and joined the conversation. No question about it, this was going to be interesting.

When my food arrived, I took my beer and burger and excused myself. Once again, I walked out to the boardwalk and sat down facing the ocean. Again, there was a long line of planes coming in from the east. Looking south-east, I saw a large ocean liner leaving the port of Miami heading out to sea. There was no breeze that evening. The surf was quiet, and a few birds chirped in the bushes along the boardwalk. Even the seagulls were unusually quiet. At dusk, I heard a low rumble of thunder. I looked to the west and realized there was a storm coming in. As I walked back to the hotel, the tiki bar was closed, the panels were down and there was no one near the pool. Inside, the guys were drinking at the bar. I wanted to join them, but I kept telling myself, "This is not what I came down here for. Stay focused and go to bed."

I turned on the TV and turned to the weather channel. The storm appeared red, green and yellow on the local radar. I soon learned why Florida is said to be the lightning capital of the world. I couldn't see the approaching storm. It was coming in from the west and my view was to the east. Bright flashes were followed by loud booming thunder. I saw waves of rain as the wind carried it toward the ocean. I was there, safe and snug in my hotel room. Except for thunder, the storm was silent. I thought about the people in the area where I was working. Huddled in their makeshift shelters, trying to stay warm and dry. I felt selfish.

It was almost midnight and I just couldn't fall asleep. I got dressed and took the elevator down to the bar. There were only a few people sitting at tables. There was only one bartender and one of our crew by the name of Cisco was having a conversation with her. I ordered a beer and took a seat on the opposite side of the bar. It didn't take long to realize that Cisco had an interest in the girl behind the bar. Somehow this made me feel out of place, so I downed my beer and called it a night. But again, I was unable to sleep. The storm was well out over the ocean now, but I could still see it when the lightning flashed. I lay there and watched that spectacular sight, still trying to fall asleep. I don't think that hotel was ever completely silent. Something would kick on, or someone would slam a door.

It's been twenty-six years and I don't remember all their names, and during the nearly six months I was there, a lot of guys came and went. However, it is safe to say that there were men from just about every state and some of them are as fresh in my mind as if it were yesterday. There were three from Minnesota. There was Robbie and his son from Seattle. Mike Thomas was from Virginia and J D from Idaho. There was at least a dozen of us from Columbus and a few from Cincinnati. And then, there were the two brothers from Texas. Freddie and Cisco. I guess I can't remember their last names, but I remember everything else about them, especially Cisco.

Cisco and Freddie were the most hard-working, kind, helpful men I had ever met. Freddie was the quiet one. He got homesick after about two months and went home to Texas. Cisco, on the other hand, had found a home away from home. He loved the atmosphere, the climate and he enjoyed the work. There were three of us who were close in age and we were veterans of the military. Myself, Cisco and Ron Lenartson. I had been in the marine corps, Ron had been in the navy and Cisco had been in the army. The three of us would meet at a small cantina for breakfast and have at least one beer each day after work. Cisco and I were single, but Ron was married and had children in Minnesota. However, he kept his marriage secret, and acted more single than any of us. He enjoyed the nightlife, the clubs and the women.

As the days passed, we began to hear more from the survivors of the storm. They all had stories to tell and those who managed to hang on to photographs showed us pictures of what their homes and their lives had been before Andrew. I remember one neighborhood in Florida city where several police officers and first responders lived. Boy did they have stories to tell. The National Hurricane Center which is in Miami, predicted a slightly different path for the storm. As late as midnight of the night before, Miami Beach was to take a direct hit. Therefore, emergency personnel were placed on duty in the predicted path. However, about two hours before landfall the storm turned slightly to the south. As brave men and women wandered through streets of cities to the north, their families huddled in bathtubs and closets as their homes were ripped from around them.

One man asked me to come to the front of his house, he had something to show me. Just days before the storm, he had had all the branches cut from the tree in his yard, leaving nothing but a stub. The tree survived the storm, but it was embedded with nails from the roofs of houses to the east. In his broken English he said, "This is why you don't want to be outside during a hurricane."

The people of south Florida are predominantly Cuban. However, there are those from Central and South America and other Caribbean islands. They all share some common superstitions and philosophies. They believe the sky is male and the ocean is female. They believe the sea will lay quietly, never speaking her mind until she is provoked. But if angered, she will rise to show her fury and her wrath. They had also chosen names for storms long before the National Hurricane Center started giving them names in the 1950s. They spoke of Andrew as if it had been a living being. An unwanted visitor who came to kill their loved ones and steal from them.

Insurance companies spray-painted claim numbers on the fronts of houses. However, there were other interesting signs. Such as, 'Damn you Andrew', 'Andrew, please stay away'. One sign addressed looters. It read simply, 'You loot, and we will eat'. In other words, they would be standing in the relief lines and there would be no one to watch over their belongings.

Anyone who was a part of the relief effort was treated like a hero. Whether you were bringing in food, hauling away rubble or helping to restore utilities, you were a hero to them. This is how you were treated, throughout south Florida. There were few who were unaffected by that hurricane. Everyone had friends, relatives or co-workers in the storm. I developed a great love and admiration for the people of south Florida.

I remember how touched I was at their willingness to share the few comforts they had. The public had been encouraged to donate non-perishable food items. Many families survived on canned beans and crackers and drank lukewarm bottled water. There was no running water. Those who were lucky made their way to distribution points where military ration meals were being handed out. All this added to our somber mood.

Chapter Four

I guess we got used to the misery that was all around us. The mood within the crew seemed to be changing for the better. I listened to their voices on the radio. Each having his own unique tech number and distinct voice. I thought, how easy it would be to mimic these guys. One morning I tried it using Charles Beam's voice. I held the talk button on my radio and in a low growling voice I said, "I-eight-thirty I-eight tuh base."

Pablo responded in his Spanish accent, "Go ahead Sharles."

It worked, but I didn't know what to say. I just held the button again, and in the same voice. "I'm sweatin."

There was a pause then Pablo said, "Ho-Ke Sharles, go ahead and um… sweat." I put the radio back on my belt and thought, *hmm, this could be interesting.*

We were required to radio in to dispatch twice each day and give production reports. Jim Geovanni would show up every morning, take a few work orders and head out. He was a part of the crew who were hanging overhead service cables from the poles to the houses, where dial tone had been restored. When these orders were dispatched, they had to be completed, and people waited at home for the technician to arrive. Four-hour time frames had to be met.

Jim Geovanni would head out with a stack of work orders and good intentions. But somewhere along the way he would get sidetracked. There were lots of yard sales as people tried to raise money. Yard sales were Jim's weakness. In fact, he had removed the spare tire from the inside of his van and tied it to the top to make room for more yard sale treasures. Scrap cable and other trash that he picked up from his jobsite were placed on top of his van. It was a spectacle to see him drive that van, with cable hanging over all four sides including the windshield. Everyone thought he was nuts, but inspectors approved his work.

When service was restored, a plastic tag called a budco tag was attached to the drop cable at the pole. The tag had numbers and letters on it that would become unique to that address and that account. Words were used in reporting letters that appeared on the tag. For example, ABC, would be, Alpha, Bravo, Charlie, or HZ, would be, Hotel, Zulu.

When a service appointment was completed, the tech was required to radio that number to the dispatcher who would record and report it to the phone company. The phone company was then required to report repairs to the Federal Communications Commission.

Throughout the day, Pablo (the dispatcher) made unsuccessful attempts to contact Jim for an update. "Base to 804, base to 804. Where are you, Yim?" And then silence. The power company had brought in help from all over the country, and within a month, they were well ahead of us. After the first month we were asked to work as many hours as we could. Another dispatcher was added and remained on duty until eight p.m. At the very end of the day is when Jim would call in his production report. Reports that were often garbled rambling and confusing. Jim never learned to use proper alphanumeric terms in reporting budco letters and numbers, he made up something as he went along. A scathing, scolding would only bring the same results the next day.

I listened and learned to mimic Jim. At random times when the radio was quiet, I would say in a high-pitch voice, "804 to bess."

Pablo would say, "Go ahead, Yim." From that point I would not give dispatch a chance to respond. I would say something that made absolutely no sense and they were sure it was Jim. I would start with a long rant, non-stop.

"I know what you want. You want some tag numbers. Do you want the one with the hanging plants, or the one with the turtles in the yard? I'll give you the one with the turtles. That's the one I did before I went up north to McDonalds. McDonalds is open you know. But there was a long line. The one with the turtles, Harry Zebra,467b3? the one with the hanging plants, Harry Zebra467b4? Then I would mumble something inaudible and go silent. As Pablo attempted to radio back, I could hear Glen Allen and the other dispatcher screaming in the background. Late in the evening poor and unsuspecting Jim would call in, further confusing everyone.

My next set of victims were Mike Karafa and Samee. I never knew Samee's last name, only that he was Lebanese. Mike's folks immigrated from Syria. The two of them often spoke in Arabic. I don't know if it was religion or politics, but it was obvious, the two of them did not like one another. Mike had a high-pitched voice and there was a slight pause between words when he spoke English. If it were possible to know that someone was assertive, or aggressive just by hearing their voice, it was Samee. Adding to that was a strong Lebanese accent. It would be so easy to impersonate those two. It would have to be a one-way conversation between myself and dispatch. I didn't want those two killing each other. I started with Samee, his tech number was 814.

"Eet-twan-foor thoo base."

Pablo responded, "Go ahead, Samee."

I said, "I haff a jop here. I cannot tuh, do thes jop. Becoss of mmm cheekens." Pablo must have been at lunch. Glen Allen answered the radio.

Glen yelled, "What are you talking about Samee?"

I just said, "There are uhhh… cheekens." Then I put my radio back on my safety belt and listened as they continued to call for Samee.

Mike Karafa was another no-nonsense kind of guy, but he was well mannered and hard-working. He was Muslim, therefore, he didn't drink or go to the clubs. He was much younger than I was, but he would stay in the field and work until I said, "That's it for the day." His work truck was a mini-van, a Chevy caravan. Like the rest of us, he carried a thirty-two-foot extension ladder. Unextended, they were sixteen feet long. The way Mike loaded his ladder left it protruding well beyond the back of his van. I said to him, "Mike, you should move that ladder forward, or attach a red flag to it. Someone could plow in to it."

He kept telling me, "Next time"

On a dark night in October, I was following him to the hotel. We were stopped at a red light, I was kind of daydreaming, not thinking about anything. Suddenly a jogger crossing the intersection attempted to pass behind Mike's truck. His forehead slammed into the ladder on Mike's truck. The impact was so powerful, I saw his truck move. The man fell to his backside, shaking his fist and yelling obscenities. Mike's voice came over the radio. "Wynn, did you run in to me?"

I said, "No, Mike. A jogger ran into your ladder. I think he's OK, but I think you'd better get the hell out of here." By this time the jogger was on his feet as Mike ran the red light and sped away. At least two more people hit their heads on that ladder before Mike decided to move it forward.

Everyone reported for work at seven a.m. However, quitting time was never established. Some guys skipped lunch and left the field at three p.m. I learned right away, that rush hour began at five a.m., and lasted until almost ten a.m. It would start up again at two p.m. and last until six thirty or seven p.m. If I stayed in the field until three p.m., I may as well work until at least six p.m. Otherwise, I would be spending my time in traffic. I listened to the frustration on the two-way radio of the guys, as they fought their way through the traffic. There were three routes that could be taken from the mainland to Miami Beach. Those who left earlier would let the rest of us know where the traffic hold-ups were. Again, those two-way radios were the most valuable tool we had.

Someone developed a home-made term for ways to cheat while making your way through traffic. The term was called 'mo-diking'. The definition, to go crazy fast, to scurry along a path, to move with quickness, hauling ass. To my co-workers, it meant drive on the curb, the sidewalk, or even the boulevard. Those guys had discovered the South Beach nightclubs and they would let nothing stand in their way in getting to them. Needless to say, this didn't go over well with the police.

By mid-October, the days were becoming noticeably shorter. I would continue to work until it became too dark to see. My greatest concern was snakes. There was hardly a day that we didn't encounter snakes. Some we knew were poisonous, others we simply didn't know. And there were so many. We often had to open underground vaults or communication cabinets and there were always snakes in them. Regardless of their size, snakes are almost always aggressive. For that reason, those of us who had the nerve to deal with them, killed them indiscriminately. Having grown up in the hills of Kentucky, I had experience in dealing with snakes.

Canals had been dug earlier in the century to drain swamps and help with flood control. There were no houses along those canals, but cross-country power and communication lines were strung on poles connecting towns. I remember working along those canals and at dusk there would be what I thought to be the pleasant chirping sound of a night bird. One evening, I asked a local what kind of bird was making the chirping sound. He said, "Those are not birds, my friend. Those are baby alligators." I was walking along one evening looking up at the cables on the poles. I heard a slight noise in front of me. I was within ten feet of an alligator. It must have been at least eight feet long. The only thing I had to defend myself with was a hammer, which I pulled quickly from my tool belt. The animal made a hissing sound, crashed into the canal and disappeared.

Through September, October and well into November, the rains continued. Almost every day, with the afternoon heating, showers or thunder storms would roll through. We had to be especially careful with lightning. The steel strand cables were perfect conductors. As they stretched for miles in every direction, lightning could strike several miles away and still be deadly. I remember once during a light rain, I saw a flicker of lightning. I realized it was time to come down from the pole. I felt a slight tug and realized that lightning had struck the strand cable, fusing the antenna of my two-way radio. I had to break it free, I also had to get a new radio.

By late October, the afternoon showers would pass through about mid-afternoon. Then the sky would become crystal clear and the humidity would drop. At dusk, I watched from the poles as a new moon appeared in the evening twilight above the western horizon. I watched that moon each night as it waxed, and its angle became higher and its glow brighter. It was autumn, but everything was lush green and tropical. Birds, frogs and baby alligators still chirped.

In the twelve years since I had left the Marine Corps, I had considered Ohio to be home. I thought about how things would be there in late October. No doubt, the trees were in their full autumn colors. The birds that hadn't migrated would be silent, and the fall crickets would temporarily fill the void with the sounds of autumn.

I thought about the home I built just a few miles west of Urbana. I thought about the long, dusty lane leading from Church Road to the circle driveway. The corn fields to the west of the house would be brown, perhaps even harvested by this time. Oak and hickory leaves would be drifted in the driveway and on the patio. But someone else would be sweeping the leaves from the deck. And someone else would have a warm, cozy fire in the stone fireplace I had worked so hard to build, just eight years before.

Chapter Five

Within a very short time, I had made some good friends among our crew. We were all in the same situation, so there was a common kinship. Everyone had a good work ethics and good attitudes. Everyone, except Charles Beam. He didn't seem to like anyone, and no one liked him. He had to be the most miserable person on the planet. If he took a seat at the bar, the whole crowd would scatter. The wait staff would cringe at the sight of him. As mentioned, he was loud, lude, crude and demanding. And it was well known, that he never showed a nickel in gratitude.

There was one man who thought Charles was the devil himself. His name was Tom Holland from Arkansas. Tom was tall, he had red hair and red complexion. In one glance you could tell that Tom was no pushover. Tom made it clear, that if Charles messed with him, he would shoot him. Charles got wind of this and confronted Tom in a crowded nightclub on South Beach. He gave Tom a violent shove, knocking him to the floor. When Tom got up, he had a pistol in his hand, it was cocked and pointed right at Charles's heart. He said, "I won't kill you here, I'll see you at the hotel."

I wasn't at the club, but this is what all who witnessed the incident were saying. I was lying peacefully in bed reading a book. What happened next took place in the room next to mine. I heard a knock at the door of that room. Then I heard someone yell, "Come on in here, Charles Beam, you fat ugly ape!"

Then I heard, "Police! Open up!" Tom opened the door and the police found the gun under his pillow. Tom was led away in handcuffs and charged with felony, possession of a firearm and a lot of other charges. Tom was in a lot of trouble. Everyone blamed Charles. He was further ostracized and rightfully so.

Nacom was paying for our rooms plus a daily per diem. However, if an individual exceeded the daily allowance, it was charged to his room and he was responsible for paying the additional charges. Soon after Tom was arrested, Charles boasted that he had gotten rid of Tom. I told him how lucky he was to be alive. But that did little to silence him. It was like every day was a celebration for Charles. He guzzled one beer after another and ordered drinks for the house. The food he ordered was the most expensive on the menu. Everyone just thought it was more of his personality flaws. You know? A fool and his money.

As for me, I continued my radio shenanigans. I even learned to mimic Glen Allen, the man who was in charge. There could be several reasons for not being able to complete a service order. For instance, a fenced yard with a guard dog. Or if the cables had to pass under a driveway or a sidewalk, the order was rescheduled for a later date. However, if an order was especially difficult, there were those who would falsely report a one of these conditions in order to pass the work to someone else. It was called, kicking the job. Jeff Fent from Ohio was one who was known for kicking jobs. He was reputed to be a cocaine addict, and he had all the symptoms. He worked very hard until about noon. Then he would become lethargic and hateful.

Fent had a unique way of speaking. He expressed everything he said in the form of a question. Except for a different address each time, every radio transmission from him sounded the same. "Eight — One — one — to base?

Pablo, "Go ahead Yeff."

"There is a dooog in the yard? And it will have to be rescheduled?"

Pablo, "Ho-ke, Yeff. Ju got thee dog in yard. Ten-four Yeff. Putting down, 'dog in yard'."

One afternoon when I knew Fent had turned off his radio and was well on his way back to Miami Beach, I called in. "Eight — one — one to base?"

Pablo, "Go ahead, Yeff."

I gave a fictitious address and said, "There's a dooog in the yard? and he bit me?"

Pablo, "Ho my God, Yeff. He bit you?"

I said, "Yes? Right in the middle of my daily duty? I was climbing the fence to get away? And he grabbed me by my aaaankle?" Then I went silent and listened to the confusion on the radio.

Pablo then said, "Ho-ke Yeff. Putting down, Ju got thee dog in yard."

I waited till things quietened down and called in again in Charles's voice. "I-Eight thirty-I-eight to base."

Pablo, "Go ahead Sharles."

Again, I gave a false address and said, "I ain't a doin' this job. Customer's looking through the fence, and they're making faces at me. Own my way to the bar."

"Ho-ke Sharles, putting down, on-way-to-bar." I have no idea what Charles Beam was doing at that moment, but everyone on our frequency thought he was on his way to the bar.

A few minutes later I heard Pablo and thought I had been busted. "Base to eight-twenty-seven."

I answered with my favorite radio voice. "Youuuu, guessed it, Pablo. And you have won this BRAND-NEW NINTEEN-NINETY-TWO — TELL 'EM JAY. HORSE AND BUGGY BUILT FOR TWO. AND THAT'S NOT ALL. YOU'RE GOING ON A TRIP. YOU'RE GOING TO SAIL THE HIGH SEAS, THE LOW SEAS, THE RED SEA, THE DEAD SEA, THE SERIOUSLY ILL SEA AND TENNESSEE."

Pablo said, "Ho-ke Wynn, ju got thee production report?"

I breathed a sigh of relief when I realized I hadn't reported in at lunch. I waited for just a short time, keyed the radio and said, "Et-O-Foor to bess."

Pablo, "Go ahead, Yim."

I gave an address and started speaking fast and rambling in Jim's voice. "I can't do this job. Customer told me to leave, said my van looked stupid, how can a van look stupid, said I was ugly, I told her to get a haircut for her kids, and trim her toenails, I finished this one, they had two dogs, two of 'em, they were nice dogs, but they pooped everywhere, the tag number is, Harry Zebra 24387. Did you get that?"

Pablo said, "No Yim. Could ju repeat the tag number?"

"Harry Zebra 23478." Then I mumbled something inaudible and went silent.

Rob Costell, was assigned to dispatch, helping Pablo from noon to eight p.m. closing. However, we still used his tech number, 807, when calling him. Rob and Glen Allen had become close friends, and Rob became Glen's assistant. Glen's tech number was 800 and he called Rob often from the field. Glen had a Virginia accent that would be easy to mimic, when the time came. His radio calls always began the same. "Aaaaght-hundred to aaaaght-zero-seven, Rob?" Almost as if he were questioning whether he had called the right person. No doubt about it, Glen would be an easy one. When the time was right.

Dispatchers, on these kinds of projects were loved and respected. They were also very busy, often working through lunch breaks. For that reason, we often bought and delivered food to them. We often helped to sort and file paper work. Massive amounts of materials were constantly being delivered and taken out to the field. Some of us volunteered to help track that as well.

Radio transmissions became very busy about every two hours as men radioed in to report completed tasks. It was between reports that I conducted my mischief. There were more than fifty of us now and I could mimic just about all of them. But my favorites were 814, Samee, 804 Jim, 811 Jeff, 838 Charles, 800 Glen, and of course Pablo. Only one person at a time could talk on the radio. When I started my tom-foolery I was careful not to let the real person chime in.

Pablo, in his broken English, often confused words and terms and it was sometimes comical. JD's tech number was 812. One afternoon I called Pablo and answered as Pablo. "Eight-twelve to base." Go ahead Yay Dee."

"Can't do this one Pablo. Gotta be bored."

"Ju are bored Yay Dee?"

"No, Pablo. The job has a bore."

"Ho, I see, you got thee sideways board Yay Dee?"

The first to speak was Rob. He said, "I must be going crazy. I heard Pablo, but it wasn't Pablo. I'm sitting right next to him and his lips didn't even move."

Soon after that I called in for Samee and answered for Pablo. "Et-twan-four thoo base."

"Go ahead Samee."

"I haff thees jop. I cannot do thees jop, there are these, umm, creeping thincs, on the ground."

"You have thee snakes Samee?"

"No, they are not tuh snakes, they are thees creeping thincs."

"Ho, you got thee frocks, Samee?"

"No, they are, ummm, leezarts."

"Ho-ke Samee, I'm putting down uhhm, leee zarts."

Then I called in using my own voice. "827 to base." Pablo. "Go ahead, Wynn.

"Pablo, I've got a little, old rodent of a dog in this yard, and one that's about, oh, he's about my size. He's a pitbull, Pablo, and he was humping my leg."

"What did you do, Wynn?"

"Well, I did the only thing I could do, Pablo. I faked an orgasm." When Pablo answered I could hear people in the background laughing, uncontrollably.

"Ho-ke, Wynn. Putting down, Or... ga... sm.

After that I thought I had better cool it for a while. But then, I remembered someone I hadn't mimicked. His name was Edwardo. He was Cuban, he spoke fluent English, but with a strong Spanish accent. He was an employee of Bell South and the project coordinator; his tech number was 801. He had a radio that was tuned to our frequency. He didn't call in often, but when he did, it was usually important, and the conversation was usually between him and Glen Allen. Glen with his Virginia accent used an extended, long 'a' sound for the word eight when calling on the radio.

I knew I was treading on dangerous ground now, but I cleared my throat and keyed the radio. "Aaaaght-hundred to aaaaght-zero-one Edwardo." Then I said, "What thoo ju vant, Gleen? I am in thee meedle off thee roid right now." Just for a few seconds I was speechless, I hadn't rehearsed what to say next. I just said, "Uhm, take two screwdrivers and call me tomorrow. Then I said, "Ho-ke, Gleen. I will take thoo screwdriferces and call ju tomorrow."

A few minutes later, the real Edwardo called Glen on the radio. "Et-toe-wan, thoo et-hundred, Gleen."

The real Glen responded. "Go ahead, Edwardo."

"I woss in thee customer yart and I hear my redio. You say sonsing about a screwdrifer?"

Glen said, "Uhh, I don't think so, Edwardo. Must be a mistake."

"Ho-ke, Gleen.

Everyone knew there was an impersonator out there, but no one suspected me. However, I knew it was only a matter of time until I was discovered. The next day was Friday and there's something that makes everyone happier on that day. It was time for the ultimate. I would start with Glen Allen. I had never done the big boss's voice before that day, but I did it so well. The following was all me and Rob. It was mid-afternoon on Friday. I keyed the radio.

"Aaaaght-hundred to Aaaaght-zero-seven Rob."

"Go ahead, Glen."

"Et-twan-four thoo base."

"Stand by Samee, Go ahead, Glen."

Et-zero-foor to bess, you want that tag numbers, the tag number is, Harry Zebra168...

"Aaaaght-hundred to Aaaaght-zero-seven, Rob?"

"Stand by, Jim. Go ahead, Glen."

"I-eight-thirty-I-eight to base. Who's buyin' the beer?"

"Shut up, Charles, go ahead Glen."

"811 to base? There's a doooog in the yard?"

"Hold it, Jeff. Go ahead, Glen."

I stopped for a moment to listen as the real people were trying to call in. Then the real Glen got through. "Hold it, hold it. I'm not there, I mean that's not me, somebody's yankin' yo chain." I had been working with Mike Karafa that day, but I had no idea he was just on the other side of some bushes nearby.

He came running, pointing his finger, yelling, "It's you, it's you." He keyed his radio and said, "This is 803, I've just discovered the mystery caller. It's Wynn Johnson." He was laughing so hard, he just stumbled to the tailgate of my truck and collapsed.

I wasn't sure what to expect when I went down to the bar that evening. Everyone was there, and Charles was the first to speak. He looked at me and said, "I don't like you. You think you're funny."

I said, "Why, Charles? I'm crushed. I'm going to have trouble sleeping tonight."

Cisco said, "I think he's funny."

Someone else said, "I think he's hilarious." Then they all began to laugh and clap. We had a wonderful time that night. The bar didn't empty until well after midnight.

Chapter Six

Things were different after that. Things seemed to have more meaning. I had found a way to make the best of the situation and my co-workers were on board with it. They smiled more, laughed more and worked harder. Everyone, that is, except Charles Beam. I didn't bother to wonder what had made him so diabolical. Looking back, I now wonder if he had been a victim of abuse as a child. But he made it almost impossible to be magnanimous with him. He would always do or say something insulting or completely unpredictable. We found it much easier to avoid him.

I always left the hotel at four forty-five a.m. each morning, and this would put me at the east end of the Biscayne Bay bridge at five a.m. sharp. From that point there were no red lights until I got to within a quarter of a mile of the warehouse. Even though the traffic was stop and go, I felt comfortable talking on the two-way radio. At five a.m. on the dot, I would key the radio and say, "Good morning, twix and tweeners. You're listening to Mo-Dike Madness radio. The weather man says, 'he sun will rise today, dark tonight with a hundred percent chance of weather tomorrow'.

Then I would create a two-way conversation mimicking the voices of two of our unsuspecting technicians. For example, Charles calling and Pablo answering. "I-eight-thirty-I-eight to base."

"Go ahead, Sharles."

"I caint come to work. I have to poop."

"Ho-ke Sharles, putting down... Sharles... poop."

Then I announced, "Tune in today at two p.m., for Mo-Dike Madness radio news."

Everyone joined in the radio humor. A situation that had looked insurmountable in the beginning was now thought to be achievable. I don't think there was anyone among us who knew what to expect when we went to south Florida. Many of us felt that we had made a grave mistake. The devastation, the heat, the insects and reptiles. Those and other issues left some guys aloof, hateful and unapproachable. Even though, we had no one to blame but ourselves. But now, we had found a way to deal with it. Even Jim Geovanni joined in the humor. I remember once when he called in a tag number. "Et-zero-foor to bess."

Pablo. "Go ahead Yim. The tag number is, Harry Zebra 17642."

Jeff Fent chimed in, "What are you going to do with that Harry Zebra?"

Jim responded. "You're just jealous of something that's got more hair on its back than you do." Almost every radio transmission resulted in clever remarks. Yet, production had increased dramatically. Those with bad attitudes were now helpful, cheerful and fun to work with.

I stopped at Publix grocery store, and picked up a copy of *Weekly World*. *Weekly World* was a newspaper that was produced weekly and filled with impossible odds and incredible, unbelievable stories. Radio call ins were quietest from one p.m. to three p.m. At two p.m., I keyed the radio and began. "Hi there, twix and tweeners. You're listening to Mo-Dike Madness news. A ninety-three-year-old woman in Bangladesh has given birth to twins. Mother and babies doing fine, but the boyfriend says, he doesn't think they're his children. The ninety-eight-year-old says he suspects his forty-eight-year-old great grandson. He says he had caught them in bed together on several occasions."

As a group I called them twix and tweeners, but one on one, I called everyone Homer. I guess it was something I had picked up from my teenage son. I think he got it from a TV show, but everyone found humor in it and everyone began to call everyone Homer.

Then I would allow a few minutes for comments while I searched for my next story. "Here's one for you guys. The Pentagon reports extraterrestrial aliens have called from outer space. They say that if we don't change our ways on earth, they're going to invade. Know what I think guys? I think they're going to get their asses kicked. They're going to hobble out of orbit with graffiti spray painted all over their spaceships."

Someone asked, "When are they coming, Wynn?"

I said, "Valentine's Day, of course."

"Here's a man who says he would be willing to wrestle an alligator for a million dollars."

I said, "Yeah, I'd wrestle an alligator for a million bucks. Why, he wouldn't even know what hit him. I would hit him with a sledge hammer, just to get his attention. As a matter of fact, for a million dollars, I would not only wrestle him I would kill and eat him." I took some comments and said, "OK, twix and tweeners. See you back at the barn."

Sometimes you just have to disconnect, extricate yourself from your troubles and just relax. I had been on the job for well over two months and I felt that a few hours away from work would help me to reenergize. The first Friday in November I decided to do just that. I radioed in to let them know I was taking off at noon. I had never made the trip midday. I was pleasantly surprised when I made it back to the hotel in less than an hour.

When I walked into the hotel lobby, I was even more surprised to see Tom Holland. He was having a heated conversation with Isabella, the hotel concierge. It seems that Tom had tried to get into his room to pick up his belongings and found that the lock had been changed. Tom kept saying, "No way, no way."

When Isabelle saw me, she waved to me and said, "Mr Johnson, could you step over here for a moment please?" I walked over, and she said, "Perhaps you can shed some light on this situation."

There are some extensive charges to Mr Holland's room, and he says he is not responsible for them."

I asked, "When did these charges occur?"

She said, "They have been accruing since mid-October."

I asked, "How much is owed for his room."

She said, "Eight hundred ninety dollars and forty-two cents."

I said, "What are the charges for?"

She said, "Mostly food and drinks, but there are also long-distance calls."

Suddenly it all became clear to me. I said, "Isabella, it's not possible for him to have made these charges. You see, this man has been incarcerated during this time."

"Then who? I could lose my job."

I said, "I'm pretty sure I know. Excuse me for just a moment." I walked away, turned on my two-way radio and called Glen Allen. I asked him to call me on the land line at the hotel's main number. The phone was already ringing when I got back to the front desk.

Isabella handed me the phone and said, "It's for you."

I told Glen what was going on and he said, "Who did all this?"

I said, "If you want my guess, I would say, Charles Beam. He's been doing far more partying than working. We've all been wondering how he could afford it."

Glen said, "Don't you say a word to anyone about this. We'll get to the bottom of this and tell that lady at the front desk not to worry. The charges will be taken care of."

It didn't take a lot of investigation for the hotel staff to confirm my suspicions. The next day, I could see Charles working about four poles away, or just over a block's distance. A few minutes later I looked again, and he was gone. Then I heard him yelling and cursing. "Somebody stole my van." Those of us who were close by ran to the street to see what the yelling was about. There was Charles, throwing his tools to the ground, cursing and kicking them. The van belonged to Nacom, and I was pretty sure it had not been stolen, but I never said a word.

Jeff Fent pulled in, and after talking to Charles, agreed to give him a ride back to the warehouse. Everyone else began to feel uneasy thinking that vehicles were being stolen. It was near the end of the day on Saturday, so everyone left the field early and headed back to the warehouse. Most of us were already in the parking lot when Jeff and Charles pulled in.

I can't find the words to describe the look on Charles's face when he saw his van at the warehouse. Glen Allen and Ron Lenartson were removing everything from it. Just then, two vehicles from the Dade County Sherriff's office pulled in. Charles jumped out of Jeff's van and ran toward his van, arms flailing, and screaming, "You all crazy. What's going on?"

Sherriff's deputies approached, and told Charles to take a seat in the back of a squad car. Charles started to protest, but one of the officers said, "Go on your own, or go in hand-cuffs." Charles got in the back of the squad car, as he looked at each of us for sympathy.

After Glen explained that Charles didn't have enough money earned to pay the charges to Tom's room and that most of the tools belonged to Nacom, Charles was released. He started walking toward the van and a deputy stopped him. He said to Charles, "You're not driving that vehicle."

Charles threw his arms in the air and said, "What am I supposed to do?"

The officer said, "Start walking."

Someone gave Charles a ride back to the hotel where he found his things in the lobby. He was told if he didn't leave immediately, the police would be called. That was the last time I saw Charles Beam in south Florida, but not my last encounter with him. I never saw Tom Holland after that either. I like to think he returned to face his day in court, but somehow, I doubt it.

Chapter Seven

It was an unusually happy mood at the circular bar that night. The bartenders were a man by the name of Matt, and a pretty blonde, her name was Nina. I called them Arthur and Guinevere. We of course, were the knights of the round bar. Every seat was taken except for the one Cisco had saved for me. I ordered a beer and Cisco said, "You can order it, but you're not paying for it. I got you covered." But Cisco wasn't the only one. I had too much beer that night and those guys never let me pay for any of them.

Cisco told me he was half Mexican and half Apache. He stood about six foot tall, dark skin and a bit of a beer gut. His hair was coal black and hung to the center of his back and his eyes were almost as black. He was soft spoken, but he had a strong Texas accent. He loved to laugh, but I don't think he could've raised his voice if he had wanted to.

One day he said to me, "Wynn, you've made this whole thing bearable. I can't explain it. When I hear your voice in the morning. I don't know, it just cheers me up. And the things you say on the radio. Where do you come up with all that stuff?"

I said, "Mostly *Weekly World*, but the rest is just good old Kentucky humor." He said, "Kentucky? I thought you from Ohio."

I said, "I didn't want Charles to know I was from Kentucky." Cisco slammed his beer on the bar. Beer spraying from his nose and mouth as he laughed uncontrollably.

A few days later I went down to the bar after work and there was no Cisco. I walked out to the tiki bar and asked, "Where's Cisco?"

Someone said, "Last time I saw him he was headed toward the beach."

I ordered two tall mugs of beer and went looking for him. I found him sitting all alone on the boardwalk. I handed him one of the beers and said, "What's up?"

He said, "Oh, I guess I can tell you. I've got a bad problem. For the first time in twenty years, I'm in love."

I said, "The girl at the bar?"

He said, "Yeah, is it that obvious?"

I said, "Only to those closest to you. You seem a little different when you're around her, that's all."

I said, "My guess is, she doesn't know it."

He said, "Yeah, she knows, and I think she likes me too."

I said, "Well, then what's the problem?"

He said, "Problem is she's married."

I said, "Yep, you've got a problem."

He said, "Yeah, she's married to some loser up in Hollywood. Guy doesn't even have a job, or anything. Did I ever tell you I was married once?"

I said, "No, I don't believe you ever mentioned it."

"Yeah, I married some German chick when I was stationed over there in the army. When I got out, I went back to Texas, rented a place and found a job as a roofer. She was to join me in one month. But when the time came, she said she just couldn't leave her friends and family. So, she stayed in Germany, we were divorced, and I never heard from her again. Broke my heart man. Nina's German, you know. And she reminds me so much of my ex-wife." Then he said, "So what do you think?"

I said, "I think it's Wednesday night and I think we need to get toilet hugging drunk."

He said, "I knew you would have a solution, even if it's a bad one. I'm with you man."

We didn't work on Thanksgiving Day. I got up early and did a couple of loads of laundry at the hotel laundry. Then I decided to take a drive. I crossed the Biscayne Bay bridge and turned left on U-S-1 south. It was only about thirty miles to Homestead, but it took hours to get there. It still looked as if the storm had happened the day before. I pulled into the parking lot of what was once a large shopping mall. There was a J C penny's and a Sears on each end of a long building, separated by smaller stores and shops. All of which were dark and without windows. Just beyond the mall and sharing the same parking lot was a K Mart. That store too was battered and deserted.

I'm not sure where everyone was going, but the area was teaming with people. They scurried about among the ruins, almost as if everything was normal. The resiliency of those people was so inspiring. Closer to the road and separate from the mall was a smaller building with lots of people gathered round it. It had been three months to the day since the hurricane. The people at that building were celebrating the reopening of the first business in Homestead since the hurricane. It was a Pizza Hut, and they were handing out free slices of pizza in celebration of the momentous occasion.

It took hours to get back to the hotel. The day had been stressful, and I didn't want to be alone. I went down to the bar and found only a few people there. Most of the guys had gone home for the holiday. I had a beer and went up to my room where I fell asleep, watching reruns of *The Twilight Zone*.

The hotel was unusually quiet for the rest of that weekend. A few of us worked Friday and Saturday of that weekend. Late autumn to late spring is the dry season in south Florida. But Saturday afternoon of that Thanksgiving weekend was different. A slow, but steady rain began to fall at about three p.m. and continued to increase as evening came. I sat on my bed and watched the rain falling on the deserted tiki bar and beach beyond.

I've always loved the sound of falling rain. I began to reminisce about days like this. The home I had built in Ohio had a balcony. I had a wonderful book collection. I used to sit on that balcony and read for hours, just listening to the rain on the roof. I remember a rainy day in autumn when I was a small child. I sneaked out of the house, went to the barn and climbed to the hayloft. I stretched out in the soft hay listening to the rain on the barn roof. I remember the smell of that hay and the cool freshness of the breeze through the open window in the gable end. It was such a peaceful repose. I'm not sure how long I slept, or how long I would have slept, if I had not heard my mother's voice calling for me.

It was late at night when I finally fell asleep. On Sunday the sun was bright, and the weather had become what one would expect in south Florida. But that was a long and boring Sunday. Old feelings of melancholy had returned to me. I think most of us spend our lives looking back and wondering if we've made the right decisions. But there are no time machines. We are forced to live with our regrets and wrong decisions. But the decisions I've made are so unchangeable, and impossible to erase. I sold my house in Ohio ten months before, when I decided to set out on this adventure. I thought once again of the quote from Walt Whitman when he said, *When the Gods want to punish you, they listen to your prayers.* In other words, be careful what you wish for, you just might get it. The only option for me was to keep moving forward.

Monday morning, I was up early. I just couldn't wait to get back to work, back with the crew, back to normal. That was the only cure. Days were much shorter at that time of year. It was still dark when I got to the end of the Biscayne Bay bridge. That's when I noticed the temperature gauge was all the way up. The truck was overheated. There is not a worse place to have car trouble in, than the state of Florida. I must admit, I was terrified. If I could make it to the top of the bridge, it would be downhill all the way to the other end of the bridge. I would cut the engine and let it roll. At least I could get off the bridge. But the traffic was stop and go. I made it almost to the top when the engine died.

The truck had a yellow beacon on top. I turned that on, and the hazard lights and opened the hood. The only coolant spilling out was from the overflow on the radiator. I knew the thermostat was stuck. It would be an easy and inexpensive fix, but it couldn't be done here on this bridge. I just had to pass some time until the engine cooled. I stepped over to the concrete safety barrier and looked over. I thought about the number of times I had crossed the bridge and I had never realized how far it was down to the water. Then a disturbing thought passed through my mind. In a single bound, one could pass over that barrier and their troubles in this world would end in seconds.

Then I looked toward the rear of my truck and noticed Mike Karafa parked behind my truck. He was talking on his two-way. With the trouble I was having with the truck, I had forgotten to turn on my radio. Just then, Cisco pulled in front of my truck. He got out and said, "Hey dude. What's going on?"

I said, "I think the thermostat's stuck. I'm just going to let it cool for a while and hopefully it'll start."

He said, "Yeah, but you could blow your engine that way. I'll hook onto it and pull you to a repair shop. There's got to be a place on highway one."

I said, "Do you have a chain?"

He said, "No man, I've got a tow strap. No respectable Texan would drive around without a tow strap."

We dropped the truck at a small, two-man repair shop. They said they would take care of it in the afternoon, but I would have to pick it up before they closed at five p.m. Cisco invited me to work with him that day, so I took the necessary hand tools and my two-way radio. We were both surprised when we got to Nacom's warehouse. There were only a few trucks there. I asked Pablo if most of the guys had already checked in and gone out to work. He said no, many of them had not come back from Thanksgiving break. Fortunately for us, those who remained were those who had been there from the beginning.

On the way to the work site, Cisco asked, "So what do you think about all these guys not coming back?"

I said, "Honestly, I think if I had gone out of Florida, I would not have come back."

He said, "You don't like it here?"

I said, "Yeah, I like it, but it doesn't feel like home."

He said, "Well the traffic's not as bad as it used to be."

I said, "I know, but it still takes two hours to travel twenty miles. I miss going for a drive in the country. I stood in line just to use a bank machine. And that was six o'clock in the morning. I miss the changing of the seasons. Not much changes here. It's sunny, hot and green every day."

He said, "So are you going to stay with Nacom?"

I said, "Of course. They have work in just about every state, and they're willing to pay me to travel. And you know? I made myself a promise that I would not stay in one place for too long. The crew I was working with in Columbus is now working in Fort Wayne. I'm invited to join them. They say the money's good."

Christmas season was an odd one for me. There was a clearing in some woods near a busy intersection. For days, workers were busy setting up amusement rides. It was called, 'Santa's Enchanted Forest'. Despite the Christmas theme, it looked like a summer event. In the shopping centers there were all the signs of Christmas. But there was no winter clothing on display and customers were dressed in summer clothing.

71

Christmas Day was on Friday. We were asked not to work that weekend and it was another long and boring three days. New Year's Eve was on Thursday. I did my laundry that morning and had some drinks with Cisco at the hotel bar. I went up to my room at about eleven p.m. I turned on the TV and found another *Twilight Zone* marathon. Just before midnight I turned the channel to see Dick Clark hosting the New Year's Eve celebration. I watched just long enough to see the ball drop to end the year 1992.

A few days later, Cisco announced that he would be moving out of the hotel. I said to him, "Aren't you going to miss talking to Nina?"

He said, "Yeah man, but I have to get away from her. She'd never leave her old man. Besides, I want my own place, man. I want to cook my own food and not have to listen to someone snoring in the next room. It's perfect man, you gotta come and see it."

It was a small studio apartment on south Beach overlooking the topless section of the beach and Cisco couldn't have been happier. Ron Lenartson, who Cisco had given the nickname, Ronbow, rented an apartment on north Beach. There were only about thirty-five or so of us left and most of them had moved out of the hotel. On the first of February 1993, the hotel announced that the hotel was sold out beginning the first of March. We would all have to be out of the hotel by then. I announced that it was time for me to leave south Florida.

Chapter Eight

It was mid-February and I didn't bother getting up early. I had to pack, and I wanted to make sure the room was in good order before I left. I had to turn in some things at Nacom, so I would make the drive once more. I turned on my radio when I got in my truck. Shortly thereafter I heard, "Base to 827."

I keyed the radio and said, "Go ahead, Pablo."

He said, "Ho-ke, guys, we'll start with the lowest number. Eight hundred, go ahead."

I listened as each tech came on to say goodbye in his own way. After Glen Allen said goodbye, I was already choked up. I keyed the radio and said, "I can't say goodbye to you guys, I'm just going to listen."

Cisco came on and he said, "I can't say goodbye either man. I'm just…" Then silence.

It was a terrible time for me. I was looking forward to leaving, but I hated to leave those guys behind. But the work was beginning to wane, and I knew it would soon be over. I had packed everything into a box that I needed to return to Nacom. I felt the faster I got in and out of Nacom the easier it would be for me. I placed the boxes in the warehouse, walked into Pablo's office, turned off my radio, handed it to him, and hurried out the door.

I drove four hundred miles the first day, and I was still in Florida. I listened to some music, but the trip was mostly sad and silent. By mid-afternoon of the second day, I crossed the Tennessee line at Chattanooga. It had been sunny the entire trip until then, but at that point, the clouds stretched as far as I could see. From west to east and north it was like driving under a shroud. I thought to myself, "*Welcome back to the cloudy midwest.*

I stopped for gas in Knoxville. The wind was blowing, and I couldn't believe how cold I felt. But I had been through months of hot, sunny weather. The heat had started in early June the year before in Ohio. I went from that to the south Florida heat. Mark Twain once said, "The coldest winter I ever spent was summer in San Francisco."

I say, "The hottest summer I ever spent, was winter in south Florida."

It was late at night when I pulled in at the Olentangy Inn of Columbus. I could see at first glance, it was no Howard Johnson. But it was close to the five-day training seminar I had to attend. I needed to keep myself occupied for the next couple of weeks until a project got underway in Cincinnati. The room had an outside entrance. I only took what I needed for the night and cranked up the heat. But the temperature in the room had been turned down to fifty and I didn't think it would ever get warm in that room. Everything in that room felt cold. The floor, the table, the walls and worst of all, the bed. It should not have been that bad. The temperature outside was thirty-one and tomorrow's temperature would be in the mid-forties. But Miami had been in the low sixties, to the upper eighties.

The next day, I was happy to see some people I had worked with the summer before. There was Eric Abbott, Ralph White, Mark Leffler and Bill Debose. I met some new people as well. There was Jeff Euki and his wife, Barbara, who worked as a dispatcher for Nacom. There was Chuck Sexton. He boasted of having been a member of an elite army group. But I swear to you, he was the most fragile, soft, feminine guy I had ever known. He got a sliver from a shovel handle and you would've thought his hand had been cut off. But he was fun to work with and he had a good outlook on life.

No matter how I dressed or how hard I worked, I couldn't seem to get warm. The Olentangy had a restaurant/lounge and the crew would always meet there for drinks after work. But again, the last thing I wanted was a cold drink. But as the days passed, I finally began to acclimatize. However, the almost constant cloudy weather was depressing.

The first Sunday in March, I checked in at the Morning Side motel just off I-275 in the Cincinnati suburb of Forest Park. When I reported for work, I was pleased to find Chuck Bixby. He was the man who had overseen the large project I had worked on in Columbus the year before. Chuck was a good manager and easy to get along with. I was assigned a brand-new machine and other equipment for drilling under roads and driveways. My task was simple. I was to drill horizontally under roads, driveways and other obstacles, place one-inch pipe under them and move on. A crew would come later to place cables through the pipe.

As mentioned, Cincinnati is a beautiful city, yet it's large enough to provide whatever you're looking for. There were times in early March when there was just too much rain to get any work done. That was tough for me. Work has always been therapeutic for me and without it I felt lost and inadequate. I just sat in my room looking to the west, watching the traffic on the interstate, just waiting for the rain to stop. There were more sunny days by mid-March, and on those days a light jacket was comfortable. The trees still hadn't shown any sign of spring, but lawns and golf courses that had been brown were turning green.

I enjoyed the work, and southern Ohio is a place where seasons are evenly balanced. Spring began on the twenty-first of March and the weather was warm. If you've never been in Cincinnati on opening day for baseball, then you should add it to your list of things to do. On the fifth day of April 1993, the Cincinnati Reds took on the Montreal Expos. Stores and shops were closed and everyone who could fit into Riverfront Stadium was there. Even though it was Monday, a lot of folks thought it strange that we were working on opening day.

There was a morning radio talk show that was hosted by a popular disc jockey by the name of Jim LeBarbor. I listened to his show each morning. He always had some interesting topics. There was a movie that was popular during that time. It was called *Indecent Proposal*. It stared Demi Moore and Woody Harrelson. It was about a young newlywed couple who was offered one million dollars by an eccentric (played by Robert Redford) for having his way with Demi for one night. LeBarbor was taking calls from women and a few men to say if they would or would not accept such a proposal. I was surprised to hear how many women said they would do it for less.

The weather was perfect by the first week in April. The grass was incredibly green, the trees were getting green and the birds were singing. I had just gotten to my room when the phone rang. It was Carl de Vault from Nacom's main office in Columbus. He said, "Wynn?"

I said "Yes?"

He said, "Boy, do I have an offer for you. You ever been to Minnesota?"

I said, "Yes, I have. Three years ago, last December and it was cold."

He said, "Well this is not December. We just took over a huge contract up there and we need all the help we can get. Not too many guys as footloose as you are. It would mean some cash bonuses. Are you listening?"

I said, "Yeah, I'm listening, but that doesn't mean I'm interested."

He said, "Well you'd better think about this one."

I said, "Carl, it's cold up there."

He said, "Noooo, I was just up there. It was sunny and temperatures were in the forties and fifties."

The next morning Chuck Bixby asked me into his office and said, "Carl call you?"

I said, "Yes he did."

He said, "Well I would hate to lose you on this job site, but the thing in Minnesota is a big deal for Nacom. Could mean a lot of money for you."

I said, "Who's going to handle the work here in Cincinnati?"

He said, "As you know, Nacom's got a lot of presence here in Ohio. But most of these guys are family men. They don't want to go out of state."

Carl called me again the next day. He said, "Well have you thought about Minnesota?"

I said, "All right, Carl give me the grizzly details."

He said, "It's a cable TV contract. Installation and MDU, multiple dwelling units. There is a ton of mainline and electronics to be placed. Damn good money in that. I've been up there for the past couple of weeks. The man running the show is some hotshot who has been working for HBO down in Caracas, Venezuela. He needs a second in charge if you want that position. There's a lot of guys going up there from here in Columbus, but I don't know how long we can count on them to stay. I think you know most of them. Let's see, there's Jerry Beckley, Chuck Sexton, Brian Marksbury, L P Muncy, Tom Givens, and Mike Kelly. There are a lot more, but I can't remember their names. We'll pay for your travel, your motel and bonuses. You'll get a cash bonus when you get there and a bonus every thirty days for six months."

I said, "Carl, I'm more interested in a project I heard about in San Francisco."

He said, "That doesn't start until the first of June. We don't expect you to stay in Minnesota forever, just help us get this thing off the ground."

I asked, "So when will all this take place?"

He said, "A convoy is leaving here Saturday morning. So, what do you say?"

I said, "I will head up the MDU team, for an additional salary above my regular pay. But I don't want to be second in charge. And I will leave from here in Cincinnati. Doesn't make sense for me to come all the way to Columbus. Indianapolis is only a hundred miles, from there it's a hundred and fifty miles to Chicago, then Minneapolis. Tell them I'll be there in a couple of days."

Chapter Nine

I just couldn't believe I let them talk me into it. But on Sunday April 11ᵗʰ 1993, I loaded the last of my things in the truck and got under way. It was a bright morning. Flowers were blooming, and the air had the smell of freshly mowed grass. I took the outer belt (I-275) south to Aurora Indiana and headed west on Interstate 74 toward Indianapolis. I would try to make it to Madison Wisconsin then stop for the night.

When I got to Indianapolis, I took the outer belt, Interstate 465 north then turned north again onto Interstate 65 toward Chicago. I stopped at a truck-stop for gas at Rensselaer. As I was pumping gas, I saw a man stagger across the parking lot and climb into a semi. It was a large truck with a sleeping compartment and I thought he was going to crawl into bed and go to sleep. However, I was shocked when I saw a smoke coming from the exhaust pipe. I couldn't believe what I was seeing. When the truck began to move, I thought perhaps he was going to the parking area behind the building. But he circled around to the street, then right down the ramp onto the northbound side of the interstate. I hung up the nozzle and rushed inside. I took a quick glance for a police officer in the restaurant then went to the counter. There were people in line, but I said, "Excuse me. Did anyone notice the guy who just drove away in that semi?" Everyone looked at one another but no one spoke. I said, "Listen we need to call the highway patrol. There's something wrong with him."

The girl behind the counter said, "Give me a minute, I have the number."

When it was my turn at the counter, she dialed the number and handed me the phone. A woman's voice said, "What's your emergency?"

I said, "I'm at the truck-stop at I-65 in Rensselaer. I saw a man stagger across the parking lot, get in a semi-tractor-trailer and head north on the interstate. There was something wrong with that driver."

She said, "So you think he was impaired? Can you describe the vehicle?"

I said, "It was a J B Hunt truck with yellow lettering."

She said, "Yes, I'm familiar with those. I am placing the call as we speak."

I got back on the interstate and continued north. After twenty miles or so, I had given little or no more thought to the man in the semi. I'm not even sure where he came from, but a highway patrol car flew past me. Shortly thereafter, another patrol car, then a sheriff's deputy, all with beacons and sirens on. A few miles further, all traffic was directed into the right lane. It was stop and go for the next few miles, then I saw the J B

Hunt truck in the median. It had jackknifed, but remained upright. Police had a man in handcuffs. I had seen a lot of bad things on the road, but that one, it seemed, had turned out OK.

Chicago is always teaming with life. I got on the Kennedy Expressway and drove past world famous landmarks. On the left, I saw Comiskey Field, home of the Chicago White Sox. To the right, was the Sears Tower. The building that had been, for a time, the tallest building in the world. Even at a distance, it appeared to stretch into the clouds. After stopping every few miles to throw change into the tollbooth baskets on the northwest tollway, I passed into Wisconsin.

It was well after dark when I drove past Madison and stopped for the night at a place called Lodi. It was cold and windy. I kept hearing Carl's voice saying, "It's nice up there. Temperatures in the forties and fifties." I looked up and saw no stars, and again I wondered how they had talked me in to this.

The next morning was still overcast with no sign of spring whatsoever. I left interstate 90 at Tomah, and onto Interstate 94. I sign read 'Saint Paul 148 miles'. I saw some snow on a hillside and told myself it had been artificially made for a ski slope. But a few miles further, I saw a pond and it was still frozen.

Nacom's office was in the Minneapolis suburb of Maple Grove. I walked in and introduced myself to the manager and was pleasantly surprised when Ron Lenartson walked in, saw me and yelled, "Homer!"

We shook hands and I said, "Small world."

He said, "Yeah, I'm not the only one. Take a look at this." We walked over to the window and outside was an old Chevy van with the spare tire on top and scrap cable spilling over every side. I knew it was Jim Geovanni. He said, "There's one more from the Miami crew." We walked back to the warehouse and there was Charles Beam.

Chapter Ten

It snowed off and on the first three days I was in Minnesota, and there were still, what I called parking lot glaciers. Snow can be pretty, but not after it has been plowed and pushed into piles and mixed with salt and sand. And after all, this was mid-April and the stuff should be gone by now. Didn't spring begin in March in Minnesota like rest of the country? However, I was in Minnesota and I was going to make the best of it.

A couple of days later I pulled into the parking lot at Nacom to find it full of trucks with Ohio plates. I walked in and there were a number of familiar faces. Jerry Beckley, Chuck Sexton, Tom Givens Brian Marksbury, Mike Kelly, and LP Muncy. I didn't know the rest, but they had all been cable TV installers in Columbus. The two whom I could relate to most, were L P Muncy and Tom Givens. Muncy and I had worked a mainline project in Columbus the summer before. Givens had worked in the dispatch office. I soon found out why. He had no driver's license or vehicle. He had ridden to Minnesota with LP, but he asked if he could work with me, until he got his situation straightened out. I thought he was a bright and likable fellow, so I said, "Sure."

With the locals who had been hired and the guys from Ohio, we got the project under way with about forty men, a full-time dispatcher, by the name of Sherry Donnelly, and a night dispatcher, Lisa Brooks. We were assigned two-way radios and tech numbers, mine was 595. From that point everyone answered to their tech number or Homer.

The company we were contracted to do the work for had been a mom and pop company that was bought out by a larger company from somewhere in New England. The new company wanted obsolete cable and electronics replaced, which included the entire outside plant. They were also running sales adds to sign up new customers. That's where the installers came in. I was to form a team to replace overhead main cable and electronics.

I was careful not to choose from the guys from Ohio. They had been brought in specifically to do home installation. Another reason was that I didn't think any of them would stick around beyond the first thirty-day bonus. I did make one exception. Charles Beam literally begged to work on my team. He wanted no part of cable TV installation. Charles had experience, but I was concerned about his climbing. The thirty-two-foot ladders we were using were rated for two hundred and twenty pounds. Charles weighed well over three hundred pounds.

The Ohio crew struggled from the beginning. The only city they had ever worked in was Columbus. And in the Twin Cities, it's impossible to travel in a straight line without running into a lake. Streets are intermittent. If they end at a lake and you still haven't found the address you're looking for, then you simply have to drive around the lake to where the street begins on the other side. Having experience with reading maps would have saved them a lot of frustration and confusion.

I couldn't get them to understand that, and after just a few days, they began to disappear. It helped a lot when we discovered a supper club called the Lookout just a few blocks from Nacom's office. Inside, it resembled the taverns in the blue-collar district of Columbus. Outside, (yet undiscovered due to the cold weather) was a patio and yard, complete with horseshoe pits. The Lookout became a place to congregate after work and it proved to be a godsend. It was a place to work out such problems as how to navigate. However, there was one problem that was insurmountable. Many of them were homesick.

The Lookout was a family-owned business. It had been built on a farm at the top a hill, by Bob Canaan and his mother. It was so named for its view of downtown Minneapolis about fifteen miles to the south-east. It was in its second generation of ownership when we came along. Among its many features were good food and a happy hour that ran from three p.m. to seven p.m. The long happy hour, did however, pose a problem. Guys wanted to quit early in order to take full advantage of it and that was just not the nature of our industry. Every installer was expected to accept late calls that were scheduled from five to seven p.m. Those who worked on my crew were exempt from late calls as our work was unscheduled.

However, I was in Minnesota to work, so I worked late anyway. Tom Givens was riding with me which meant that he had to work late as well. That did not set well with him. He would call for someone to come to my job site to give him a lift back to the motel. If there was no one in the area, then he would sit in the truck and sulk. As days went by, he began to demand to be taken back to the motel at five p.m. One day when I had worked until six p.m., I got in the truck and he was angry and began to curse. I stopped the truck and told him to get out. He said, "What the hell are you talking about? I don't even know the way back."

I only responded, "Get out." He did, and I drove away.

The next time I saw him, he was riding with L P Muncy, helping with home installation. I'll use a line or two to describe LP. He was fifty years old and average in height. He had a large nose and ears. His hair had once been dark, but it was now salt and pepper. His complexion was extremely red. Some would call it whiskey flush. Originally from Kentucky, he had a strong southern accent, and the more he tried to make a point, the higher the pitch of his voice.

One evening after work, I knocked at the door to his room. He called out, "Come in." I stepped into his room and LP was sitting on the bed leaning against the headboard. He looked to be exhausted. I asked how it was going. He said, "I can't make no money at this."

I said, "What's the problem?"

He said in a screaming high-pitched voice, "I drove a hundred and fifty miles today. Seemed like I was going in circles."

I asked, "Are you letting Tom navigate?"

He said, "Yes."

I said, "That's the problem LP. Tom can't read a map."

The next day LP began to watch for familiar landmarks. One of which was a large statue of a cow in front of a butcher shop. That evening I stopped at his room to find out if things had improved. He said, "I think you're right, the man can't read a map. I finally told him, I said, 'Tom! if you take me past here one more time, I'm going to get out and bust the head off that cow'. Next thing I know, we were all the way up on Bass Lake Road. I said, 'Tom, what are we doing way up here when we need to be way back down south'. And you know what Tom said to me? He said, 'LP, you told me not to take you past that cow again'.

Meeting at the Lookout was about the only thing keeping the Columbus guys in Minnesota. The workdays for them appeared to be ending earlier each day. Driving back to Nacom's office late one afternoon, I saw Brian Marksbury. He'd been pulled over and the police had him in handcuffs. He was being charged with driving while intoxicated. I never saw him again.

Lisa Brooks turned twenty-one on June 11th and everyone met at the Lookout to help her celebrate. The party ended around ten p.m., but some of the guys decided to stay till closing at midnight. Jerry Beckley missed a curve on the way to the motel and rolled a new Chevy caravan. He was pulled from under the van with severe burns from the exhaust system. He recovered, but the van was totaled, and it belonged to Nacom. In just one night, Jerry Beckley had gone from a highly motivated, top-notch installer to no license, a drunk driving charge and fourteen thousand dollars in debt to Nacom. He would soon disappear as well.

As hard as we tried, there was no stopping the guys from heading back to Columbus. One or two each day until only three of us remained. Myself, LP Muncy and Charles Beam. Charles was doing well until he threatened one of the dispatchers with bodily harm and was fired. LP announced that he too was leaving in mid-June and I couldn't talk him out of it.

Brian Blakely asked if I would ride back to Columbus with LP and pick up a new van to replace the one Jerry Beckley had wrecked. I would receive a cash bonus for the trip and I agreed. We left early on a Saturday morning. LP Began to talk and he didn't stop.

When I went to Miami, LP had gone to Fort Wayne for a three-month project. That crew found a favorite spot to hang out. It was a strip joint called Boom-

Boom's. Through three hundred miles of Wisconsin, that's all LP wanted to talk about. What he was leading up to was that he wanted to stop there on the way. I protested. I said, "LP, I really don't want to go two hundred miles out of the way just to see naked women."

He said, "But these women are special, they're the most beautiful women in the world."

I said, "Don't you realize those women have husbands or boyfriends at home? And don't you have a woman at home waiting for you?"

He said "Yeah, but I'm not serious about her. I think she's cheating on me, but I'll cechim. I'm going to sneak around back and wire the back door shut. Then I'll bust through the front and cechim."

I said, "Sounds like a plan LP, but drop me at the Olentangy Inn first."

He said, "You know? You cain't trust a woman. I had one and she was driving me crazy, so I shot her in the foot. I told her to go to the hospital and tell them the gun fell off the mantel and shot her in the foot. And I told her if she came back, I would shoot her in the other foot."

I said, "Whatever happened to her, LP?"

He said, "She left town. Bad foot and all."

We were on interstate 65, southbound, when LP took the Merrillville Indiana exit, then turned east. I knew, he was determined to go to Boom-Booms in Fort Wayne. I made myself as comfortable as possible, went to sleep. When I woke up and looked at my watch, it was almost midnight. I realized LP had parked in the alley behind the place. Had we not gone so far out of the way, we might have been to Columbus, at least to Dayton. To say the least I was angry. I walked in through the backdoor. The bouncer gave me a look, but he didn't put his hands on me. I found LP all the way to the front of the place. There was no bar and no tables, only a stage and chairs. Men and a few women were sitting as close to the stage as possible. They were looking up at the stage like hungry dogs at the supper table waiting for table scraps. There were four fireman poles and colored lights shining on the stage. The girls wore high heels, nothing on top and just enough on the bottom to stuff money in to. Beauty is in the eyes of the beholder, but let's just say I didn't behold any beauty.

I didn't even sit down. I just said, "LP we have to go — now!" He knew I was angry. He just got up and followed me out. I said, "Are you OK to drive?"

He said, "What do you mean?"

I said, "Are you drunk?"

He said, "They don't serve alcohol in there."

I said, "How do they make money?"

He said, "They charge to get in."

I said, "They didn't charge me anything."

He said, "That's because it's closing time. You wouldn't have gotten me out of there if it hadn't been closing time."

It was like frames and flashes. When I left Ohio, it was fresh and spring green. It was only June but compared to Minnesota it looked to be midsummer. The van was parked on the street in front of Eric Abbott's house. He was a good friend and I would've loved to knock at the door and at least say hello. However, it was early on a Sunday morning and I was afraid of disturbing him and his family.

Ohio had been home for a long time. I had built my first home here and watched my two children grow to be adults. I had watched the dark fields turn green, then brown and dark again so many times. I found the keys under the floor mat and started the engine. The tank was full, and I knew if I didn't leave at that moment, I probably never would.

Chapter Eleven

After about a week in Minnesota, and just when I thought spring would never come, I opened the curtains to a sunny morning. It was such a different day, in so many ways. I felt happy and invigorated. I headed straight to the job site. The other guys showed up a short time later, they were in a happier mood as well. There was some frost that morning, but by noon, the temperature was perfect. I don't think I've ever seen snow melt so fast. Rivulets ran from every parking lot and along every curb. The sky was dark blue, and the robins were singing. It was like nature had suddenly answered a wake-up call.

The weather was perfect for the next few days, then it began to rain. The rain and the snowmelt made its way downstream, toward Iowa and other states along the Mississippi River. At one point, in 1993, the Mississippi River was nine miles wide in Iowa. But the rain didn't bother me, I love rain. And when it wasn't raining the weather was perfect. It was strange to me. Rain would be pouring and just a short time later the sun was bright, and the sky was blue.

Lilac trees grow wild in Minnesota and in early June they were in full bloom, with deep purple and lavender pods of blossoms. Flowering shrub and fruit trees were blooming a few days later, then the spring flowers. One day, I got my first mosquito bite in Minnesota. From that day on, you could not work outside without insect repellent. Minnesota has a reputation for mosquitoes, but the record rainfall made it worse than ever.

As the weeks passed, we were able to hire more local help. But I have to say it was different. I was never able to capture the camaraderie and team spirit we had in south Florida. It seemed that no one wanted to do the work as a career, but only until they could find something else. They wouldn't think of working manual labor till they retired. They wanted to get back into college, get a degree and live an easy life. As much as I appreciated that, it only made it difficult to hire permanent help.

Ron Lenartson was running the home installation department and I was in charge of MDU, or outside plant issues. However, I was called upon to troubleshoot for both departments. I was pulled and pointed in every direction. I love to work hard and stay busy, but it was beginning to take its toll on me. Then one day, I got a call on my two-way radio. A new hire was asking for help. When I got to the address, I saw a truck with magnetic Nacom signs on it, but I didn't see the driver. I rang the doorbell and there was no answer, so I walked around to the back of the house.

I found him under a patio that was about four and a half feet above the ground. He was attempting to bury a TV service cable. The poor guy was bent at the waist, soaked in sweat, with crushed mosquitoes stuck to his face. He looked to be in his late forties, to early fifties. He had a shovel in his hand and had dug a ditch about a foot deep through the wet clay. When he saw me, he leaned on the shovel and exclaimed, "Damn! Can a guy make any money at this?"

I said, "Sure, but not the way you're doing it."

Just then a handsome black man joined us, and as black people are fortunate not to show their age, I had no idea how old he was. He held out his hand and said, "My name is John Morris, that disaster under the patio is Richard Walter."

Richard said, "Gee, thanks a lot."

I shook John's hand and said, "I'm Wynn Johnson."

He said, "We know. We were told that you were the man who could show us the ropes."

I said, "My first question is, are you going to stick around? Because, if you don't give me, at least a verbal commitment, then I'm not going to waste my time or yours."

Richard said, "I'm very excited about this."

John said, "Me too, if I can make a living at it, but that Ron fellow said we should be able to complete six to eight of these in a day."

I said, "You can, after you've been taught how to do it correctly.

"First, I want to tell you a little about the industry. First of all, they're always going to paint a prettier picture than it really is. If a project manager tells you the work is going to last for years, then expect it to last for months. If he says months, then expect weeks. Don't drink and drive, because no one is going to hire you if you don't have a valid license. Be careful of your tools, because the people you think you know will steal them. Don't let anyone look down on you for being a contractor. Contractors built this country, especially the communications systems. If you work hard, work late when you have to and you're willing to travel, you can make a lot of money."

They both said yes to all the above and we walked back to where Richard had been working. I said, "The first thing I want you to ask yourself is, are you burying a cable or a storm sewer?"

Richard said, "I don't follow you."

I said, "Let's fill in this trench and I will show you how to use a straight-bladed shovel to open a slit, without digging a trench."

John said, "That's great, but don't they make machines that will do this?"

I said, "Sure, but a machine would cut through the underground sprinkler system, the underground power cable to that shed in back and the natural gas line running to the gas grill on the patio. But leave the cable

TV service cables to the young beginners. I would like to invite you guys to join my MDU team. If you're interested, we can discuss it over a beer this evening at the Lookout."

You would've thought I had given those two men winning lottery tickets. They couldn't have been happier, but probably not as happy as I was. Then I called Mark Coons on the radio and asked him to join us. Mark had been in the industry for several years, as a residential installer. He too was excited to learn the mainline aspect of the industry.

It was about six p.m. when we met at the Lookout, but there was still three and a half hours of daylight left. It was late June, during some of the longest days of the year. Minnesota is known for deep blue sky and bright sunshine and we had both that evening. The birds had quieted to chirps and tweets, but there was enough of a breeze to keep mosquitoes at bay. Visibility was endless that day. The city was alive with the sound of rush hour and the sky was busy with planes going into or out of MSP International Airport.

We didn't discuss work. It was more about getting to know one another. We ordered food and we drank beer. Richard and I won three out of five games at the horseshoe pits. At nine p.m., we called an end to the meeting. The fun and games were over for now. The company we were contracting for, had just approved an almost unlimited budget for their cable TV systems in apartment buildings.

We met at a large apartment complex in the Minneapolis suburb of Brooklyn Center. I had the core of my team, then another experienced installer showed up with eight apprentices. His name was Larry Hoff. He and his team were willing to complete the work that had to be done inside the apartments. That was perfectly agreeable to me. That meant that all my work would be outdoors.

The complex was called, Four Courts. Brooklyn Center is very close to inner city. It was said to be a high crime area and we were told to be careful, that all work should end before dark. I didn't see anything to worry about. There were four large L-shaped buildings with about an acre of land in between. It was a beautiful courtyard shaded by tall ash and maple trees and a playground in the center. To me, it appeared to be a happy place where happy, screaming children played. It was days before we were able to answer all their curious questions.

It was a cool and fresh morning and the last Monday in June when we got underway. A trench was opened to place cables from one electronic terminal to the next and from one building to the next. With two-way radios crackling and twenty thousand feet of cable stretched across the courtyard, everyone was happy, and everyone was working.

At the beginning of the third week on the job, there was a late afternoon thunderstorm that halted work for about an hour and a half. That meant that we were late in picking up tools and equipment to end the day. It was about seven p.m. when two cars turned the corner of the street adjacent to the apartment complex. Then one car pulled alongside the other, blocking the street. A third car stopped in front of the other two, and the driver honked his horn. Apparently, he wanted to pass. We didn't hear any voices or arguing, only the sound of gunfire as the people in the side-by-side cars blasted away at each other. Then one car sped away and the other made a U-turn. But before they left, they fired a shot into the windshield of the person who wanted to pass. The local news made little mention of the incident. They only reported that rival gang members had a shoot-out in Brooklyn Center and police were looking for suspects.

In the fourth and final week of the project, we heard a gunshot. The only strange thing about it was that it was early in the morning. I won't say that we had grown accustomed to hearing gunshots, but aside from that, it was such a quiet morning. Perhaps a little too quiet. There were no children at the playground. It didn't matter who, or why, the shot was fired, it only took the sound of gunfire to put these parents on edge.

There was no mistake in the fact that we had heard a gunshot. I could tell from the concussion of the blast. However, black people in poor communities tend to keep their troubles to themselves and the police were not called to investigate.

There were open-fronted sheds that housed the garbage dumpsters, one for each building. About mid-afternoon, Mark Coons and I took some scrap cable to one of the dumpsters. Behind the dumpster and in the back of the shed, we saw someone's feet. At first, we thought it was a homeless person taking a nap. But the fellow wasn't homeless, he was dead. There was a pool of dark coagulated blood beneath his head and some blood had run from the corner of his mouth and dried on his cheek. There was a handgun near his right hand. He was a black man, with a salt and pepper beard. My guess would have been that he was in his upper forties. There was a sense of sadness and oppression at Four Courts. I have to say, I was glad when two days later we finished the project and moved on.

I remember working that summer of 1993, but for the life of me, I don't know how it could have passed so quickly. The manager, Brian Blakeley, was celebrating his thirty-fifth birthday, so a surprise party was arranged at the Lookout. It was a Friday afternoon and we stopped working at three p.m. Almost everyone who worked for Nacom was there and some people from the cable company. I have to think there were at least fifty people at the party. It was an outdoor event, with food, drinks, music and horseshoe competition.

It was a beautiful afternoon, but the mosquitoes were horrendous. However, Mike Canaan, of the Lookout family, brought out some sort of fogging device. He sprayed the outer perimeter of the yard and we had no further problems with mosquitoes. Everyone was happy, and work was the furthest thing from our minds. In fact, there didn't appear to be any worries on anyone's mind. But then, two unexpected guests arrived.

Brian's brother and his long-time partner had flown in from Boston. They were Keith Blakeley and Ben Kamila. Brian became very emotional and what everyone thought would brighten the party, had an opposite effect. Brian only stayed at the party for a short time after Keith arrived. The three of them had just a little food and then they quietly walked to Brian's car and drove away.

Everyone had noticed that both visitors looked to be weak and frail. Brian had just celebrated his thirty-fiftgh birthday. Everyone thought Keith and his partner were much older. In fact, Keith was older, but only by three years. You see, Keith and his partner were suffering acquired immune deficiency syndrome, or AIDS Within a matter of a few short months both men would be dead.

The party continued, however, the mood was a somber one. Groups of people sat quietly at tables and tried to think of happier things. Looking out over the landscape, the trees were beginning to show their autumn colors. The sun glistened on the tall glass buildings of downtown Minneapolis. But the sun's angle was much lower now, and at seven p.m., it was setting. Soon there was a chill in the air, it was late September, and the summer of 1993, had ended.

In October, we started work on another large apartment complex with twelve hundred apartments. It was called Century Court and it was in the suburb of Brooklyn Park. It was another place where we were warned to work in groups and be out before dark. But again, it was advice that was unheeded. And who wouldn't be deceived? The buildings were well-kept, tan colored three-story brick, probably built in the 1960s. The hallways and common areas were freshly painted with carpeted floors. There were enough large trees to cover the entire grounds with shade. There was an in-ground irrigation system that kept the grass green, except in the playground area. Freshly fallen leaves had been gathered into piles where children ran, jumped and played, after school. The smell of dinner being cooked drifted through the screens of open windows.

However, things became quiet as children disappeared at sundown. Once again, we were close to finishing the project when we arrived one morning to a large police presence. It was said to have been a drug deal gone wrong that caused a clash between the Crypts and the Bloods. Members of one gang broke in to an apartment on the garden level of one of the buildings. However, it was already too late when they realized they were in the wrong apartment. A middle-aged man was shot to prevent him from being a witness.

The gang went to the matching apartment in the next building. But the rival gang had been tipped off and they were waiting in the dark. As soon as the window broke, the gang inside the apartment opened fire. Several gang members on the outside were wounded but managed to escape. But the man leading the way was shot in the head and died at the scene.

Chapter Twelve

As for myself and my crew, we had had enough of this inner-city work. It was late in October; the work was beginning to wane and I felt it was time for me to move on. However, Brian Blakeley and the dispatchers were begging me not to go. Brian said, "Listen, take a break from this, get out of town for a few days and regroup. I have a project up north that's perfect for you."

I said, "Up north? I thought I was up north. What've you got Brian?"

He said, "Trap change, in three different towns. Warren, Minnesota, Devils Lake, North Dakota and Fergus Falls, Minnesota, in that order."

Traps were small cylindrical devices that were used to control cable TV pay channels. Negative traps were used to block channels such as home box office. Positive channels were installed to enable channels such as Cinemax. These devices were installed high on the utility poles, to prevent customer tampering and theft of service. Each active customer line contained one to five channel traps. I only needed one helper, so Richard Walter volunteered. John Morris did not want to go, he stayed behind to work home installation until Richard and I returned to resume the MDU work.

Warren is in the north-west portion of Minnesota, just over three hundred miles, from the Twin Cities. It was mid-October when we left, and the fall foliage was at its peak. Most of the five-hour drive to Warren was done in the dark. We were a little dismayed the next day to find there were no leaves left on the trees in Warren. The weather was cold, and it was like going from a warm, bright autumn, to early winter. It only took a few days to complete what had to be done in Warren, then we headed west to Devils Lake. The distance is about one hundred and twenty miles, and mostly open plain. The only trees were in the small towns along the way. Devils Lake was a farm community at the crossroad of state highway 20, and US Route 2. The population of the town was about six thousand.

It was a peaceful looking place with small to moderate sized homes. Many with full-length porches with swings facing streets where tall elm and maple trees lined the boulevard. Hay bales, corn bundles, squash and pumpkins had been placed in front yards to celebrate the harvest season. Some pumpkins had been carved into jack-o'-lanterns to celebrate Halloween.

The weather was sunny and cold, but tolerable for the first couple of weeks. Working high on the poles along the edge of town, I could see for miles out over the yellow plains. Then one morning, we came out of our motel rooms to find about two inches of wet snow on the ground. The snow had stuck to the trees and the overhead cable lines. It was pretty at first, but then a tempest wind blew in from the northern plains knocking the snow from everything that was overhead and right down our collars.

I had nothing to complain about. It was the kind of adventure I had dreamed about as a child. I had always had a fascination with the north. Growing up in a large family, my parents bought groceries in bulk. I remember a picture on a large sack of flour. The brand name was Polar Bear. It was a picture of a polar bear adrift on an ice flow in the glow of the northern lights. I used to stare at that label in amazement. When I was older, I read adventure stories about hunters lost in the northern wilderness, or their encounters with wild animals. And now that I was in the north, I was just as thrilled as I had imagined I would be.

The snow hadn't melted when we finished in Devils Lake and headed for Fergus Falls. I knew that area probably wouldn't see the ground again without snow until late April. The ground was covered with snow all the way to Fergus Falls. We finished up in Fergus Falls and headed back to the Twin Cities on Tuesday, two days before Thanksgiving.

I walked into Nacom's office about mid-morning on Wednesday, the day before Thanksgiving, and except for the dispatcher, the place was deserted. I said, "Hi Sherry, how's it going?"

She said, "Slow. In fact, I only have two guys in the field and they only have one job each to report. As soon as they call in, I'm locking up and I'm out of here." I wished her a happy Thanksgiving and I left. I had moved from the Red Carpet Motel in Maple Grove to a to a motel near Rogers, just a few miles further west. The reason was that the place in Rogers had a kitchenette, complete with a stove and microwave. I wanted to be able to cook my own food for a change.

Richard lived with his elderly mother in Coon Rapids, Minnesota, a northern suburb of the Twin Cities. His father lived near Rapid City, South Dakota. He had a sister in Greely, Colorado, but no other relatives in Minnesota. However, having lived in Minnesota for more than twenty years, he had lots of friends and plans for the weekend. I called on the two-way radio to see if anyone wanted to have a beer before the bars closed. When there was no return static, I knew that every radio was off. Everyone had scattered to the winds. They had gone to spend a relaxing and festive weekend with friends and family. Suddenly, I felt alone. I felt very alone.

There was a bar just a couple of blocks from my motel. It was called the Municipal bar and liquor store. The locals called it, the 'Muni'. They sold burgers and tavern pizza on regular business days, but not on that day. They were closing at six p.m. I bought a six-pack and walked back to my motel. I turned on the TV and turned to the Weather Channel. There was a snowstorm headed for the Twin Cities, and we got it. When it was over, there were eight inches of snow on the ground.

I had nothing to do but be lazy. I watched TV and read books. Late Friday afternoon I opened the curtains and the sun had already gone down in the south-west. The red glow of the sky over the freshly fallen snow was a beautiful sight. I could hear the traffic of interstate 94, as people rushed home to be with their families. I thought I too would take a drive through the country and do a little exploring. It was dusk when I walked out of the motel and a bright full moon had already risen in the eastern sky. The air was clear and frosty. This brightened my mood, somehow the moon had always had that effect on me.

I got in my truck and headed west on long country roads. If it looked as if I were coming to a town, I simply turned the other way. I passed farmhouses with smoke coming from chimneys. I imagined folks reclining in front of cozy fireplaces reading books. I saw houses with large living-room windows with a soft warm glow from shade lamps. Then I turned down a road where I saw no houses in sight. The moonlight was so bright, I turned off the headlights and drove down that road taking in the beauty of the countryside. I was so warm and comfortable in that truck, I just wanted to keep driving and gazing at the snow-covered meadows, the moonlight and the starry sky, unspoiled by the artificial light from the truck.

But it felt as if it were late, even though the clock on the dash said seven thirty. That's because of the long, late autumn nights. It had been nearly three hours since sundown. So, I turned and headed back toward the motel. Just a couple of miles from Rogers, I came to a small tavern called The Riverside Inn. It was appropriately named for it stood next to a bridge that crossed the Crow River. There were only a few cars in the parking lot, so I stopped for a beer.

There wasn't as much as a breeze that night when I stepped out of the truck. The parking lot had been plowed, yet the snow squeaked under my feet as I walked toward what looked to be the main entrance. When I walked in, I found the place to be dimly lit and quiet. A bar stood directly in front of the door, and to the right, was a larger room where the few patrons were playing cards. A middle-aged lady placed her cards face-down on the table and walked behind the bar. "What can I get you?" she asked.

I said, "Well I'm new in Minnesota. What kind of local beer do you have?"

She said, "How about a Grain Belt? It's brewed in southern Minnesota."

I said, "Sounds good. I'll try one."

I expected a lot of questions, but she handed me the beer and walked back over and rejoined the card game. I took my beer and walked past the people playing cards to a table by a large window facing the river. There was not enough light in the place to spoil the moonlight. I had a great view of the winding Crow River. Ice was beginning to form along the edge of the water and it glistened in the moonlight.

I could tell the place had been there for a long time. When my beer was almost gone, I got up and walked around the place. There were posters of the Minnesota Vikings, the Minnesota Twins, and Minnesota North Stars on the wall. I thought, that's a little sad. The Minnesota North Stars moved to Dallas last spring. On the next wall was a poster of the Minnesota Lakers. Then I knew the place had been around for a long time. The Minnesota Lakers had moved to Los Angeles to become the LA Lakers in 1960. Then I came to a wall with enlarged photographs, some were black and white, and some were color. At the very top was an eight-by-ten black and white photo of a man and woman who looked to be in their sixties. They were standing in the parking lot next to a 1958 Ford sedan, with Riverside Inn painted on the side. All the cars shown in the photograph were from the 1950s.

I walked back to the bar and ordered another beer. This time the lady asked, "So where are you from?"

I said, "I came here last spring from Cincinnati." Then she asked, "What brings you here?"

I said, "Work."

She said, "Well you won't stay, it'll be too cold for you."

I said, "Is this place always this quiet?"

She said, "No. It's usually packed. But everyone's hunting, or they're home with their families."

I said, "Looks like this place has been here for a while."

She said, "Yeah, it has. A farmer and his wife built it right after World War Two."

I said, "It's a nice place. Almost like a step back in time."

She said, "We know. We like to keep it that way."

Chapter Thirteen

We completed one more apartment complex in the western suburb of Plymouth. However, heavy snowstorms kept coming two and sometimes three per week. It became so deep, it was just not practical to continue. And on Thursday, the 23rd of December we shut down until after the new year.

I had met a girl who worked as a waitress at Denny's family restaurant in Brooklyn Park. She was twenty-eight, pretty and fun to be with. Her name was Cindy Yost. She was single and had never been married. She grew up in a good Lutheran home in Pine City, about an hour and a half north of the Twin Cities. She seemed to enjoy my company as well. She would call me unexpectedly and say, "Let's go out and do something." However, there was also something unusual about her. She never had time for me on weekends. We'd both make plans for a weekend date and then I would call her and there would be no answer. Or we would plan to meet somewhere, and she wouldn't show up. For all these reasons, I never took her seriously, nor did I allow a steady relationship to develop. In the beginning I would call her and ask if she would like to meet for a meal, or to have a drink. She would say yes, then I would wait for an hour or more and realize it was another no show. I didn't get upset about it. I just figured that's how Cindy was. But when days would pass and I hadn't called her she would call and say, "Why haven't you called me? I've been worried sick?" I just couldn't figure her out.

No one could deny the spirit of Christmas in Minnesota. The snow was deep and getting deeper by the day. There were Christmas lights everywhere and people hurried about as if it were sunny and seventy degrees. No one seemed to pay attention to the cold, or the icy roads. But it was lonely in that motel room. Christmas was on Saturday and the following Tuesday I called Brian Blakely and asked if he would join me at the Lookout for a drink.

We met that afternoon and I told him it was time for me to move on. He said, "Wynn! You're leaving me high and dry here."

I said, "Now listen, Brian. I told you in the beginning, that I wouldn't be here permanently. And work has practically ended here."

He said, "Listen, Randy Carpenter is running the show in Saint Louis and he's begging for help. Run down there and help him out for a couple of months and there'll be more work than you can handle in the spring. At least stay within my base."

I said, "What does that mean?"

He said, "I've been promoted. I am in charge of North and South Dakota, Minnesota, Iowa and Nebraska. I have some huge projects coming in 1994, and I need you to help me to bid them."

I said, "All right, I'll leave for Saint Louis next week."

I called Richard Walter and John Morris and asked them to join me once again at the Lookout. It was Friday, New Year's Eve. They were there waiting when I got there. After a couple of beers and a lot of small-talk John said, "I'm having a blast, but is there a reason for this meeting?"

I said, "Yeah, I just wanted to say goodbye. I'm leaving next week for Saint Louis."

Richard said, "Is there work down there?"

I said, "Yes, but it's inner city."

Richard said, "I've got nothing going on. I don't mind going down there for a couple of months."

I said, Good, I'll call Randy Carpenter first thing Monday morning and tell him to arrange another room. How about you John?" John became teary eyed and said, "I'd love to join you two clowns, but I've got a shaky marriage already. I can't go."

The three of us shook hands, embraced, said Happy New Year and I promised I would see John in the spring. But somehow, I knew I would never see him again. I drove to my motel, parked the truck and walked to the Muni for a six-pack. I decided to have a couple of beers before going back to my room to be alone. However, the place was so noisy with the regular crowd, I felt out of place. I walked to my room and turned on the TV. I watched Dick Clark host the New Year's Eve celebration at Times Square in New York. I watched the ball drop, and I watched as 1993, came to an end.

A few days later, I was headed south on interstate 35 South. I would've liked to have said goodbye to Cindy, but I figured it was time to turn the page so, I made no effort to let her know I was leaving. There was a strong wind blowing from the west and snow was covering the highway faster than plow crews could remove it. A pale sun was shining, but the temperature was seventeen below zero. I was near the Iowa border when I experienced a sun-dog for the first time. It takes a low sun angle and ice crystals in the air to create the right conditions. A sun-dog, looks like three suns in the sky, with a rainbow-like reflection surrounding all three.

The route I was taking was interstate 35 south to Kansas City, then east on interstate 70. Nacom's office was in Saint Louis. However, a motel had been arranged for Richard and me in the western suburb of Saint Ann near Lambert International Airport. I thought I would never make it to Des Moines. Visibility was next to nothing and every time I passed trees, or an embankment that blocked the wind, the truck would lurch to the left and almost out of control.

After I passed Des Moines, there was very little snow on the ground, but the strong wind continued to blow. Then, for about fifty miles, there was no snow. Then on the hills about fifteen miles south of the Missouri border the snow fell hard and fast. Vehicles were off the road, in the median and upside down. When I reached Kansas City and turned east, there was no snow and the wind was hardly noticeable as it was blowing from the west and I was driving east.

When I reached the motel in Saint Ann, there was no snow on the ground. But it was twelve degrees, the wind was blowing, and it felt colder than ever. My room faced west and there was a cold draft coming through a crack around the door. I called the front desk to complain and they brought me blankets and told me to sleep with my clothes on. The noise from the interstate was terrible and when a plane took off, the entire building shook. But I was a tough old ex-Marine. I just considered it to be another adventure.

I started working the next day. Richard had not yet arrived. It was not a good area of town. There were about twenty installers. My job was to hang overhead cables form the utility poles to the houses or apartment buildings. I was the only white man in the workforce and I was told not to go inside of any structure. The work was assigned according to postal zip codes. The manager, who was also black, pointed out the most dangerous codes. We were to make sure that we were out of those codes before dark.

One evening when we were checking in at Nacom, a man said in an excited voice. "What time is it? If I'm not home by six p.m., my wife has me declared legally dead." There were buildings that looked to be abandoned, yet people lived in them. It was place where children roamed the streets. Sometimes they went to school and sometimes they didn't. Large, hungry guard dogs walked from corner to corner of fenced yards. Trampling dry, frozen grass into the frozen ground and crawling into gutted appliances for shelter.

Holes in windows were stuffed with rags, or they were boarded over and covered with heavy black plastic. Installers could not do their work inside without flashlights, even during the zenith of the brightest days. No one was trusted to see what went on inside. The good people didn't want the bad people to see them. Much like a child hiding under the blankets. At sundown, any sounds that were friendly and civil faded and was replaced with loud music and parties. Soon cheerful voices became angry as an occasional gunshot rang out. I have watched ambulances race to a house, only to sit and wait for police to come and make it safe for them to do their job.

Crooked installers had for years sold services. They would hook up the service for a one-time fee and that party would have service until they were discovered and disconnected. Therefore, whenever a worker climbed a utility pole he was asked, "Whose cable y'all disconnecting?"

Or if they were looking to pay the one time fee, the standard question was, "Y'all running any specials?"

Richard arrived about three days after I got there, and he wasn't sure what to think. He was the kind of fellow who treated everyone the same, at the risk of being misunderstood. I told Richard repeatedly, "Tell them you are connecting service. You are not disconnecting anyone." But Richard was known for speaking his mind.

He was working on a pole when a man came out and asked, "What do you think you're doing?"

Without even looking down to see who had said it, Richard replied, "Trying to do my job."

Suddenly there was a loud pop as splinters flew from the pole just above Richard's head. He scurried down the pole as quickly as he could and called my tech number, which in this case was 442. He said, "442 you there?"

I was on a pole a few blocks away and I could tell from the tone of his voice, something was wrong. I turned down the volume on my radio and said, "Go ahead 44."

He said, "Dude, I just got shot at, I'm through with this. Where are you?" I told him and a couple of minutes later he pulled in. I radioed dispatch and asked them to call the police.

I asked if he saw the shooter. He said, "No. I had my back to him and I didn't want to see the son-of-a-bitch. I just wanted to get the hell out of there."

I asked, "Is your ladder still on the pole?"

He said, "Yeah, and it can stay there for all I care."

I said, "We have to get the ladder. Nacom will take three hundred dollars out of your check for it. We'll wait for the police." We waited for almost a half an hour, then we moved to within sight of the ladder. We didn't see anyone, but we didn't see the police either.

We waited for just a few more minutes and when we didn't see anyone, we moved closer. The utility pole run along the alleys and I kept thinking we were going to be ambushed from any window. Then I just took a deep breath and said, "This is it, Richard. We're going to get that damned ladder. We pulled alongside the pole and loaded the ladder. It was eerily quiet and mid-afternoon when we headed to Nacom to check in.

We both stormed into the office and said, "We're done."

The manager said, "Hold on a minute. What's the problem? What did the police say?"

I said, "The police didn't show up and I don't think you called them."

He said, "I sure did, I swear it. Sometimes they get busy and they don't show up."

I said, "You're telling me they don't respond to attempted murder?"

Richard said, "Come on Wynn, I need a drink."

When I got to the motel that night, the man at the front desk said that someone had been repeatedly calling me. Not long after I stepped into my room, the phone rang. It was Joe Govern, senior vice president of Nacom. I had never met him, but he spoke to me as if he had known me all my life. He said, "Hey, dude, what's up? This is Joe Govern. I'm the…"

I cut him short. I said, "I know who you are. What can I do for you?"

He said, "What would it take to keep you in Saint Louis?"

I said, "Joe, I'm not the one who got shot at. You should call Richard."

He said, "I'm told that if you stay, he'll stay."

I said, "What are you offering?"

He said, "A cash bonus and higher wages. Let me talk to the board of directors and get back to you tomorrow."

I said, "Why is this so important?"

He said, "The cable company you're working for there is Time Warner."

I said, "Yeah, I'm some dumb, but I'm not plumb dumb. I know who we're doing the work for."

He said, "Time Warner, formerly Warner Brothers, makes everything from cartoons to top rated, blockbuster movies. They're also one of the largest cable companies in the world. Nacom has over sixteen hundred sub-contractors and employees working for them. We know Saint Louis is a tough one that's why we're willing to make it worth your time."

I knocked at Richard's door early the next morning and asked him to join me for breakfast. We met at a local truck-stop and he was clearly agitated. I told everything Joe Govern had said and he wanted no part of it. We were at that table for an hour and a half. Richard spent more time trying to convince me to leave, than I spent trying to get him to stay.

Richard had a habit of calling everyone, 'Dude'. But he was more poignant than I had ever seen him, and I was a little taken aback when he called me by name. He said, "Wynn, listen. Except for out here in Saint Ann, you're the only white person I've seen in Saint Louis. That's a bad area down there where we're working. Those people don't want us there."

I said, There's a lot of good people down there, Richard, they're just so impoverished."

He said, "I know that, but we're trying to make things better for them and they think we're there to take something away. I'm not staying, and I think it's a mistake for you to stay. I think if you stay, you're going to get hurt, or worse." We shook hands in the parking lot and I followed him to the interstate. I watched as he turned onto the westbound ramp of interstate 70, and once again, I felt completely alone.

Chapter Fourteen

I fell into a routine and tried to make the best of it. I had breakfast at the truck-stop every morning at five a.m. and walked into work promptly at six thirty a.m. I had a micro-wave in my room and a small refrigerator/freezer. I went to Walmart for groceries on Thursday evenings, did my laundry on Sunday mornings and watched football in the afternoon. When the football season ended with the Super Bowl, I had to find other ways to occupy myself on Sunday afternoon. I went to a science museum, and one afternoon I went to the Gateway Arch. However, the line to go to the top was too long so I didn't wait. There was a movie theater at a shopping mall nearby. Sometimes I would see a late movie.

Two days after Richard left, I was working in an alley behind Martin Luther King Boulevard. It was never quite daylight when I climbed my first pole, but it was mid-morning and just as dark as ever. Then I noticed sleet bouncing off my jacket sleeve. The temperature was thirty-two degrees, and I was sure it would change to rain, but it didn't.

Within minutes the sleet was coming down hard and had already coated the ground. By three p.m., about three inches had fallen and there was no let-up. I thought

I'd better knock off early and make my way to the motel. I had only gone about two miles west on interstate 70 when the traffic stopped. It took a half hour to travel the next mile. The eastbound traffic was also at a crawl. Visibility was so poor it was hard to see from one side of the interstate to the other. There was even an occasional flash of lightning.

Headlights from oncoming vehicles appeared to float ghostly by. I thought about the contrast from where I was and where I had been just one year before, when I was in sunny south Florida. Then I thought about all the miles in between. I thought about the double spring of last year, beginning in Cincinnati, then the Twin Cities.

Finally, I saw flashing lights and saw that it was only a fender-bender, but three cars were in the median. It was only twelve miles from the work area to the motel, but it was dark when I finally got there. The next morning, I looked out to see the truck covered in a thick coat of ice and sleet. But it was a bright morning and that's the first time I had seen the sun in days. I turned on my radio to let dispatch know that I would be late and there was no answer. I knew it would take hours, perhaps all day, to make the roads safe to travel. I chiseled the ice from my truck, took my Louis Lamour novel and went to the truck-stop. I didn't go to work until the next day. It was another sunny day, but there was at least eight inches of sleet on the ground. I had never seen anything like it. It was almost like the sleet would splash as I walked through it.

It did, however, make the day seem brighter. But as the days passed it was not so pretty. Only main thoroughfares had been cleared. Alleys and side streets remained coated in a thick layer of ice. There was the occasional sound of tires spinning as people attempted to go to work or run errands. Alleys became littered as overfilled garbage cans and dumpsters spilled onto the ground. Only footpaths led from houses and apartment buildings to the streets. The same guard dogs wore trails along the fences and walked in their own waste. I remembered a line from an old song, *This town don't look good in snow*.

I was working in a place where it didn't appear that spring would ever come. But on Monday, the first day of March, I got a call from Brian Blakely. There was a trap change in three small towns in southern Minnesota. I told the local manager in Saint Louis I would be leaving at the end of the week. I had worked in Saint Louis for nearly two months. I felt I had given Nacom ample time to hire a local workforce.

I could've taken the interstate all the way back to Minnesota, but I had a few days, so I decided on a different route. I was going to take the scenic route along the Mississippi River. My plan was to drive west on interstate 70, to Saint Charles. From there I would take highway 79 north-west to Hannibal, then US 61, all the way to Saint Paul.

The snow and sleet had melted, the sun angle was much higher, the grass was turning green and I even saw a few robins. I'm sure the people of Saint Louis love their town, but paradise doesn't exist in a lonely world. The further I drove north the better I felt.

The scenic byways along the Mississippi River are something everyone should see. The roads twist and turn with the river. Small towns lay along the banks where grain elevators stand ready to transfer their cargo. To folks passing by, they're just another building, blocking the view of the river. However, hundreds if not thousands of people are employed directly or indirectly as a result of them. Farm mortgages are paid, equipment is bought, and college tuitions are met. Then there are the people on the barges and those who receive their shipments. Where millions of tons of grain and the fruits of countless farms have been loaded on barges for who knows where. Train tracks run the length of the river on both sides. You're hardly out of sight of one train, when another comes into view.

There are hills and bluffs on both sides of the river. The two-lane highway often climbs to the top of the bluffs where cliffs had been blasted away. Time had erased the evidence of the blasting as cliffs that were once white, are now gray and the road is as old as the history of the automobile.

Parks and scenic overlooks have been created where travelers can stop to take in the view, or to let the engine cool. It was easy to imagine a young family out for adventure. The station wagon loaded with children, blankets and a picnic basket. Perhaps a teardrop trailer in tow. The children marvel at the scenery as Mom and Dad spread out the blankets and the picnic. Every overlook has its favorite spot to read, and to daydream. Or to look out over the mighty Mississippi River as it carries the waters of a thousand rivers and streams never-ending, through the ages, to the sea.

I stopped for the night at a small motel in Dubuque, Iowa. Dubuque was another town that had been built as a result of the river. Before there were highways, rivers were the only mode of travel through the densely forested woodlands of America. Dubuque had a history that pre-dated the Black Hawk war of the 1830s.

In the motel lobby were eight-by-ten photos proudly displayed. It was pictures of a film crew that had stayed there during the filming of *Field of Dreams*. It stared Kevin Costner and James Earl Jones. The movie had been filmed on a farm a few miles west of town.

As strange as it sounds, I had trouble sleeping. I had gotten used to interstate noise and low-flying planes. It seemed to be a quiet little town, even during rush hour the next morning. I went to a local diner for breakfast. I was seated next to a group of what looked to be farmers. They all wore cover-alls and scratched up leather boots.

I could hear every word they were saying. In fact, I think everyone in the place could hear them. There were six of them and three of them thought it was going to be an early spring and other three disagreed. Then they began to put forth their evidence. The proof was in everything from farm animals, to birds and wooly-worms. Then it became obvious that three of them were democrats and the other three were republicans. Those guys had no doubt been friends for life. And they had been meeting here every morning for as long as the place had been in business. Trying without success to resolve issues that can never be changed, such as the weather and politics. I wasn't sure if it was going to be an early spring, but a bright warm sun shining down on that beautiful river sure made it look like spring. But I still had two hundred and fifty miles to go. My concern was how early spring would be in Minnesota.

Chapter Fifteen

There were still snowdrifts and parking lot glaciers in Minnesota. I loaded boxes of channel traps onto my truck and drove about ninety miles south to the small town of Waseca. Waseca was located between two lakes. Loon Lake to the west and the smaller of the two. Clear Lake was to the east and almost as big as the town. I chose to start the trap-change in Waseca. There was still snow on the ground, but the utility poles were located along the boulevard and easy to access. In fact, it was one of the easiest jobs I could remember. There were four to six overhead cables running to each pole. I simply looked at the work orders to determine what services were needed. I then climbed the poles, with everything I needed to complete the work and was done with each location within minutes.

My work was completed in about a week and a half. The next town was about another hundred miles south-west. It was the city of Worthington. It was a much larger project, so I called Richard and asked if he and John Morris would like to join me. They joined me in Worthington and together we completed that project in just over two weeks. Next stop was Fairmont. Those projects kept coming, the weather continued to improve and soon it was April.

I got a call from Brian Blakely on the Friday before Easter. He wanted my help in bidding two large projects in eastern Iowa. We were to leave on the afternoon of Easter Sunday. The first was a veterans' hospital in Iowa City. It took five hours to make the drive and we took Brian's company car. It was a brand-new Ford Taurus. I did the driving and to me it was a quiet, smooth ride, but Brian didn't think so. He complained of hearing a noise coming through the glove compartment. I couldn't hear a thing.

Brian and I had become close friends. He was an interesting fellow. He had a master's degree in communications from Ohio University. He was born to wealthy parents and grew up in Sandusky Bay just west of Cleveland. For several years he worked as a producer for Home Box Office (HBO) in Caracas, Venezuela. He met and married a young lady there by the name of Julie. She was a pretty lady, but I had never seen such a temper. I jokingly warned him that Lorena Bobbitt was also from South America and he didn't see the humor. He said, "Listen, don't even joke about that. Sometimes, I'm very much afraid of her." So, his marriage to Julie was a tumultuous one to say the least.

We got to Iowa City and checked into a Motel 6, then met for dinner at a bar/restaurant across the street. We talked about upcoming projects. We were to present our findings to Nacom's main office in Columbus. It would be complete with estimated labor cost and a bill of material. The veterans' hospital was the smaller of the two projects. We completed that bid in only two days. The other was the University of Northern Iowa at Cedar Falls, just north of Waterloo. The bid for that could take as long as a week and a half.

Both projects were being done for TCI (Telecommunications Incorporated) the largest cable company in the world. The University of Northern Iowa would be a massive undertaking. There had never been cable service at the university. Thirty-two hundred outlets along with a main cable signal plant would have to be built from scratch. The work would have to be done between June 1st and September 1st while the students were away for the summer.

It's been a lot of years, but I still remember some of the names of the buildings. I believe there were seven large dorm room buildings and various classroom buildings. I remember Loren Hall, Campbell Hall and Bender Towers. The towers were two identical high-rise buildings. I believe they were twelve story and would prove to be the most challenging.

We completed the bids, faxed everything to Columbus and I rejoined John and Richard who were now working in Albert Lea. As the weeks passed, I had put the Iowa projects out my mind, until I got a call from Brian on Memorial Day weekend. TCI had awarded both the university and the hospital to Nacom. However, Nacom accepted only one of the two — the university.

130

Memorial Day was on May 31st. Brian asked if I could be in Waterloo to meet with the local manager from the cable company, his name was Bill Mangrich.

Bill was always friendly and helpful, but he had done nothing in his career except home installation. Therefore, he knew very little about what it took to make a cable system work. He assured me that everything that Brian and I had listed on the bill of material had been ordered. He also said, the only material that had arrived was cable. The electronics were on back-order and should arrive soon.

There were a few faculty members who worked through the summer and some students who attended summer classes. The university had some claim to fame. There were some star athletes and so forth. However, faculty members were proud of one of their professors, who had written a bestselling novel. My daughter had given me a copy of the book in 1992, and I read it when I was in Florida. The professor, who had since moved to Texas, was Robert James Waller. The book was called, *The Bridges of Madison County*.

Two days later, a crew arrived from Columbus with massive directional boring machines and excavators. They were there to place main cables from what is known as the head-end. This is where dishes receive signal from transponders on orbiting satellites. They would install the cable from that point to the center of the campus. From there it was up to me, and a crew of twelve guys from Nacom's office in Omaha.

The crew from Omaha was led by a brute of a man by the name of Calvin. He was a tall muscular fellow who didn't have much to say. When I met them, he was the only one who spoke. He just said, "We were told, that you would show us what to do." They brought with them a large hammer drill called a Hilti. We were sure to need it, for all the floors in those buildings were reinforced concrete.

There were tunnels beneath the campus where sewer, water and ducting had been installed. We called them steam tunnels because of hot water pipes that were hot enough to blister if you touched them. Those pipes also made it extremely hot in the tunnels and that's where a large portion of the work had to be done. The main signal plant would be constructed in the tunnels. Outlet cables would pass from the tunnels below and up through the cavities of interior walls to reach upper floors. The work would require an enormous amount of drilling.

Due to his height and strength, there could not have been a better person to operate the drill. Calvin never seemed to tire. I would simply mark the spot and he would slam that drill bit to the spot and blast a hole through the toughest of wall or floor. He never complained about the heat in the tunnels, or the noise of the drill. The dust mixed with sweat, and at the end of the day, Calvin looked as if he had been rolled in flour. Other members of the Omaha crew used smaller drills to attach the cable to the concrete walls of the tunnel.

Even though the main cable is three-quarters of an inch in diameter it was quite delicate. A dent or kink and that section of the cable would have to be replaced.

We were near completion of the outlets and the main cable, however, the electronics had not yet arrived. Another day or two and we would be at a standstill, with nothing to do but leave and come back when the parts arrived. I got to my motel in Cedar Falls around five p.m. and I heard the phone ringing when I got out of my truck. I was sure that whoever it was would hang up before I could get to it, but the phone kept ringing. When I answered, it was Sherry Donnelly, the dispatcher.

I could tell she was upset as soon as I heard her voice. She said, "Wynn! What are you doing? When are you coming home?"

I said, "Home? Sherry, what's this all about?"

She said, "No one's told you? Julie chased Brian into the street, trying to stab him with a knife. She's in jail and we don't know where Brian is. Things are falling apart."

I said, "Well, where is Ron Lenartson?"

She said, "Ron was fired a week ago for false billing. I've been running things, but the cable company wants to know what's going on."

I said, "Sherry, we've done about all we can do here for now, but I can't leave until I let the Omaha crew know that I'm leaving. I'll put Calvin in charge and leave here by eight thirty a.m. Call Greg Moske, he can help with things till I get there."

The guys from Omaha knew the remainder of what had to be done. I turned over the supplies that were on my truck, shook hands with them and got under way. As I'm sure I've mentioned, I don't like endings. Regardless of what it is. Whether it's a movie, football season, or worst of all saying goodbye. When I said so-long to those guys that morning, I knew I would never see them again.

I looked at the map for the fastest route and then headed north on route 218. I would follow it to the small town of Floyd, then turn west to Mason City, then north on interstate 35, to the Twin Cities. It was eight twenty a.m. when I left Cedar Falls. It was Tuesday morning, June 21st, the longest day of 1994. It was a warm and extremely bright day. Fields of corn, wheat and soy beans stood in the dark fertile land along the Cedar River Valley.

Expert farmers knew exactly what to do to keep their crops growing fast and fruitful. They knew just when to till, when to plant, what to spray and when to harvest. There's an old saying among farmers. 'Knee-high by the 4th of July'. Meaning that if the if the corn stood knee-high by the 4th of July, the crops would have a good yield. Well, they had nothing to worry about. The 4th of July was still two weeks away and the corn was already waist-high.

People in big cities mistakenly think that life would be boring in small towns. Folks in small towns have evolved to enjoy their brand of entertainment as much as those in the cities. The people in small towns enjoy good, wholesome, harmless lives. I saw lots of evidence to support that fact as I drove across the farmlands of Iowa that day.

In Waverly, there was a pancake breakfast every Sunday morning at the Lutheran church. There was a fish-fry at the American Legion in Charles City. There was a softball tournament to be held on July 2nd, 3rd and 4th. I saw several signs posted along the roads for that one. It would no doubt be the event of the year. A time for rival schools to compete. Or perhaps a way to prove all the bar-room boasting of the used to be high school jocks. It was interesting to me that seemingly, the smaller the town, the larger the events.

The speed limit through those small towns was twenty-five miles per hour. But that made it safer and it gave one the opportunity to as they say, "People watch." You had to be especially watchful as ten, or twelve-year-old boys flew through intersections seldom looking from side to side.

Ball-bats tucked under their arms and oversized, over-used gloves hung from handlebars. Excited to get to the park and start their own adventures in glory. Housewives laboring to drag boxes and stacks of household goods into the garage, or onto the driveway. The result to be a long day of reading, as neighbors visit and search for bargains. But it's all in good fun. Because when the sale ends and the day is done, she will count perhaps as much as thirty dollars in profit.

It was early afternoon when I reached Faribault. Now in radio range, I called Sherry and asked her to call Brian at home and ask if he would meet me at a place called Alligators in Plymouth. She said Brian would be there in one hour. I found Brian sitting in a back corner and even in the dim light he didn't look good. He asked, "How's it going?"

I said, "Fine, you're the one we're all concerned about. Can we move to a table by the window? It's like a cave in this corner."

We moved closer to a window and talked briefly about the university project. I asked about Julie, and he said, "Julie's in the Hennepin County jail, charged with attempted murder."

I said, "Wow, that's pretty serious."

He said, "Yeah, tell me about it. I've got an attorney. He's trying to get the charges reduced to assault, or something. Right now, we're just trying to get her out of jail."

I said, "No offence sir, but aren't you the one who had her locked up?"

He said, "No, I'm not the one. She chased me into the street with a knife and one of the neighbors called the police. Look, I don't know what to do. I love that woman. The lawyer says that she might get off easy if she agrees to some sort of treatment. He also says that if she doesn't, she could lose her citizenship and be deported. Not too many people know about this. Will you keep it under your hat?"

I said, "That's why I asked you to meet me here. No one knows us here."

He said, "There's one more thing you need to know. I'm moving to Omaha. I will recommend you for my position here if you like."

I said, "No, I can make a lot more money in the field, with much less headaches. But why Omaha?"

He said, "I told you I had been promoted. Omaha is going to be the test market for all of telecommunications over the next few years. You wouldn't believe how much work is going to be going on there. Among other things, US West Telephone company is building the world's first interactive phone and cable TV system in Omaha. And Nacom has the contract to build it for them."

After that, Brian and Julie slipped quietly out of town and his brother, Mark, came from Ohio to take his place. I never knew that brothers could be so different. Mark didn't have the education or the experience that could be respected. In fact, he had no experience whatsoever in the telecommunications industry. He had been installing appliances in Sandusky when Brian offered him the position. Richard called him, "The Maytag repair man."

One must have or learn certain leadership traits and principals in order to be a manager and Mark had none of them. It didn't take long for me to figure that out and when I did, I had as little to do with him as possible.

Chapter Sixteen

I turned forty on June 28th, in 1994. I never was one to celebrate birthdays and there were only a few people left at Nacom that I knew, so the event went unnoticed. It was, however, a milestone I couldn't completely ignore. I couldn't help but reflect on what life had been and what was left of it. I was in tip-top physical condition, but it was safe to imagine that I had already spent half of it.

The next time I heard from Brian was on Friday, September 2nd, the beginning of Labor Day weekend. He said, "The parts for the university finally came in."

I said, "Brian! I had put that project completely out of mind. I thought it had long since been done by another crew."

He said, "No, it's going to be up to you my man."

I said, "Well aren't classes back in session?"

He said, "They start up again on Tuesday, but that's not our fault. They didn't get us the parts, so there was nothing we could do. You'll just have to do the best you can."

I said, "What do you mean, Brian? You make it sound as if I'm going to be doing all the splicing and activation on the entire university."

He said, "You are. But don't worry, you're going to make a ton of money."

I said, "You're serious. You want me to do that entire job by myself."

He said, "You'll be fine. The only other splicers we have are in Columbus and they're busy."

I said, "Well can I take John or Richard along for a helper?"

He said, "No, neither of them know how to splice and you won't have time to teach them. Get packing. If I get time, I'll drive out there and have a drink with you."

I said, "I'm not going to have time to drink."

I was not going to rush back down to Cedar Falls. I wanted to be angry, but I didn't know who to blame. We had all summer to get this project completed and now I would have to trip over a bunch of bratty, know-it-all college kids. But having a weekend to cool down, I left early on Monday morning. It was the fifth day of September, Labor Day.

I had been seeing Cindy off and on through the summer, but I was leaving once again without saying goodbye. It was hard to remember the summers in my life. Easy to remember the beginning or the end but nothing in the middle. Summer memories were either attached to late spring or early autumn. And now another summer was coming to an end.

I had an entire day to get to Cedar Falls. The interstate to Mason City would be the quickest route but,

I chose a more leisurely one. I drove to Saint Paul and took highway 52, south toward Rochester. About twenty miles south of Saint Paul, highway 52 passes through the small village of Cannon Falls. There were two red lights on 52, in Cannon Falls. Beyond that was sixty miles of open road leading to Rochester.

It had been sunny and dry across the upper Midwest throughout the month of August. I crossed and paralleled several river valleys through southern Minnesota. There was the Cannon River, the Vermillion, and the Zumbrota. Rivers that had for thousands of years carried and deposited rich, dark soil along their banks. The only imperfection in the fields of grain were small quarter-acre size spots stunted by spring flooding. There were now, very few small farms left in the Midwest. Thousand-acre farms are the average. Just like in John Steinbeck's *Grapes of Wrath*. Small farms have been gobbled up by rich farmers and large corporations and it wasn't only in Oklahoma.

The land was a rolling landscape through southern Minnesota. Long gravel roads stretched east and west from 52. In contrast to the fields on either side, they appeared to be white in the early morning sun. Dust billowed behind cars on those roads like the condensation trail behind a jet plane. A few patches of mist floated over late summer flowers and meadows.

Passing through Rochester, I saw the white buildings of the empire that is the Mayo Clinic. Founded by Will and Charlie Mayo, two mediocre doctors and sons of a local physician, who were bold enough to try new remedies and create specialisms in the practice of medicine. The Mayo Clinic is a place where people come from all over the world for treatment of cancer and other deadly diseases.

Another mile or so, and I turned off 52 and onto Broadway, or highway 63, a route that would take me along scenic byways. Through peaceful little towns, such as Spring Valley, Cherry Grove and into Iowa. The traffic had been light for a holiday. For just a moment I thought it was Sunday and most folks were in church. But then I came to the realization that it was Monday. I kept wondering where everyone was, then it became obvious. Many houses and yards were deserted while others were alive with celebration. Driveways and even yards were full of parked cars and pickup trucks as smoke rose from backyard barbeque grills. Parents led ponies around back lots as children enjoyed pony rides. Folks played lawn darts, or horseshoes. City parks were filled with folks playing softball. Everyone was taking advantage of the final warm days of summer and that day was a perfect one. School would begin the next day and it was a ceremonious goodbye to summer and a welcome to early autumn.

I followed 63, to a little place called Artesian, Iowa, then turned west on highway 3, to Waverly, and south again on highway 218 at Waverly. I was then on familiar territory that I had seen in the spring. It looked familiar, but it didn't. Fields that were then dark green had turned to a pale green in the summer sun. Corn tassels that were yellow were now brown and the lower leaves of the corn stalks were yellow. Wheat fields had long since been harvested. Now the soy bean fields were yellow and almost ready for harvesting. Again, it was like frames and flashes. Where had the summer gone?

I checked into my motel and called Bill Mangrich and left him a message to let him know that I would be at his warehouse at eight thirty the next morning. I was there at a quarter past eight and Bill was already there. We shook hands and he said, "I would offer you a cup of coffee, but I know you're a busy man. So, follow me and I'll show you what I have done so far." Bill had all the parts organized and placed in boxes and away from other warehouse inventory. He had a copy of the blueprint tacked onto a bulletin board. I showed him where I would begin, he helped me to load my truck with boxes of material and I was on my way. It was about five miles from the warehouse in Waterloo to the campus. I felt a sense of anxiety as I made that drive. I kept thinking how I would be intimidated by those know-it-all college brats. I would be old in their young eyes and they were sure to poke fun and look down on me. To think of me as another uneducated loser working a dead-end job. I wanted so much, to return the electronics, and drive away.

I got there to a very different scene to which I had grown used to when I was here in June. Every parking lot was filled to capacity. I didn't see anyone, but I knew

142

they were there, in the classrooms and I would surely have to interact with them. There was just no way to keep a low profile and get this done. I was sure they would be quick to point out that I was the trespasser, on their territory. I was so damned nervous.

Finding no vacant parking space, I parked in a no parking zone and walked into Campbell Hall where I found a lady of about fifty years of age at a reception desk. I told her who I was, and she said, "Oh yes! We're so excited that you're here. Let me call Ernie for you. He's the head of maintenance." She made the call and a man about my age appeared a short time later. I thought it was ironic that his name was Ernie. He looked just like Jim Varney, the actor who played Ernest in the movies.

He said, "We're so glad you-all are finally doing this. We have been trying to get cable TV for these kids for years. Now what can I do to help?"

I said, "My main concern is where to park."

He said, "Do you have any road cones?"

I said, "Yes, I have two."

He said, "Perfect. Just put one in front of your truck and one behind it and park anywhere you like. We know who you are."

I had a plan for avoiding the students as much as possible. I put the main power supply in place beneath Loren Hall. There were five amps which I mounted on the walls of the tunnel. The rest of the electronics would be housed in steel lockboxes in various places beneath the buildings. I could assemble those on the tailgate of my truck at the motel. The following morning, I would take what I had assembled the night before into the tunnel and splice it into place. By early afternoon, I would return to the motel to assemble more.

Then the day came when I would have to complete what was known in the industry as activation, sweep and balance. In other words, turn it on and make it work. Much of this work could not be done in the tunnel and I began to have direct contact with the students. I was ashamed of all the bad thoughts I had felt about them. The activation took three days and I will break the editor's rule of too many adjectives in describing them. I found them to be kind, honest, hard-working, well-mannered and polite. Every conversation I overheard was devoted to learning. They were from many walks of life and I was so pleased to see such quality in the youth of America. Each day, I was excitedly asked, "Is it going to be today?"

"When are we going to have cable?"

"When are you going to make it work?"

Every time I entered a dorm room, I was asked, 'What can we do to help?' or, 'Do we need to move anything out of your way?'

It was then, that I began to see the length they would go just to get one snowy channel on a little TV screen. There were comical feats of engineering, as various antennas had been rigged. Usually attached in some way to the TV's antenna, were pop cans — strings of pop cans, sheets of aluminum foil pinched to the cable connection on the backs of TVs. Foil that had been twisted, folded and braded into chains and strung about the room. The same sort of apparatus extended through one window, in at another window to join two TVs.

Much of the activation was done on a weekend in order to gain access to dorm rooms. Within the final stages, entire buildings were activated. They all seemed to know where I was working, and I believe that all eyes were on their TV screens. As I placed small components, called forward and reverse pads, and equalizers into amplifiers, the picture would fade in and out as adjustments were made to the slope and gain. In would cause a rousing cheer, out would bring a mournful, "OOOH."

Football season was in full swing and students congregated into dorms that I had completed. Each day I received heartfelt thank yous and pats on the back. What had started out to be my most dreaded task, had turned into the most rewarding work I had done since the hurricane. I finished my work at the university on September 25th. I said goodbye to everyone I had gotten to know and headed north on highway 218. I was happy, but also sad. Another ending and another summer now officially over. I'm not even sure what made me drive north again toward the Twin Cities. Autumn would be short and whatever work was there would soon end for the season. I looked to my right and saw the first bright, full moon of the autumn of 1994.

Chapter Seventeen

I helped with installation in the Twin Cities for the next week and spent some time with Cindy. I had really grown to care for her, but she kept me in a state of confusion. I began to think the only cure was to move on. I called Brian, to find out what Nacom's next plan was for me. He said, "Things haven't kicked off here in Nebraska yet. We're still waiting for permits and plans to be drawn up. Your old buddy, Chuck Bixby, is looking for help in Indiana. Have you had any experience with satellite dish installation?"

I said, "Yeah, I helped to install one when I built my house. I helped the guy who installed one in my yard, but that was ten years ago."

He said, "That was one of those old ten-foot dinosaur dishes. This is something new. It's an orbiter that the big cable companies paid NASA to develop and deliver to space. It replaces the old Galaxy-5 satellite. It's an effort to provide cable TV service to folks in rural areas. Receiving dishes are only three feet across and can be installed in about three hours. Nacom's getting more orders for these than they can keep up with. It's called Primestar."

I had only seen Cindy once, while I was in the Twin Cities. I didn't think she would take the time out of her day to see me off, so I didn't call to say goodbye. John Morris had no interest in a career that required him to travel. Therefore, he had long since moved on. I invited Richard to join me in Indiana, but he was still bitter about what had happened in Saint Louis. So, there was little ceremony when I left the Twin Cities in the fall of 1994.

Autumn colors were once again at their peak when I left the Twin Cities and headed east on interstate 94. I crossed the Saint Croix River bridge into Hudson, Wisconsin. It was the first time I had been that far east on that highway since my trip to Ohio almost a year and a half before. Talk about mixed emotions. Part of me felt as if I were going home. Part of me felt that I had failed in Minnesota. Then I thought about my success in places such as Devils Lake, Saint Louis and the university. I reminded myself that I was doing exactly what I had set out to do.

Chuck Bixby had arranged a room for me at a motel in Beach Grove, Indiana. The city of Indianapolis is square in shape. Beach Grove is a suburb at the southeast corner of that square. I was to meet Chuck at a sports bar across the street from the motel, at one p.m. the next day. I got an early start. I wanted to treat myself to driving through Wisconsin during daylight.

Wisconsin is one of our most beautiful states. It's called 'America's Dairy'. The first hundred and fifty miles is rolling hills where farms are separated by forest. Farming has been the industry that has driven the economy there for a hundred and fifty years. Even from the interstate, it was easy to see how well kept these farms were. Sheds and barns are red with white trim. Houses and fences are neatly painted white or gray with white trim. Grounds are kept mowed, shrubs and trees are trimmed and pruned.

The autumn colors were beautiful. And the smoke from a farmer burning brush could be seen for miles. The sumac was dark red and late summer flowers were drooped and wilting. The result of the first frost and the promise of the short autumn and the long winter ahead. Herds of milk cows instinctively followed the leader in single file to the barn at milking or feeding time. I'm sure the life of a farmer is not a perfect one and their work is never done. But there's something very appealing about the security and peacefulness of never having to leave home.

Interstate 94, merges with interstate 90, at Tomah Wisconsin. They run together east to Madison, where 94 continues east to Milwaukee and 90 turns south-east toward Chicago. From Tomah, the forest become piney woodlands on both sides of the highway. There are hills and bluffs that rise from the valley floor that somehow look to be out of place. Strange buttes, plateaus and chimney rock formations are scattered through the valleys as if they'd been playthings of the gods.

The highway crosses the Wisconsin River, at a place called the Wisconsin Dells. From there the landscape becomes more agricultural again with herds of cattle and fields of grain. My intention was to stop for the night at Merrillville, Indiana. At that point I would be clear of the rush and hurry of Chicago. Interstate 90 becomes the north-west tollway from the Illinois border passing O'Hare International Airport to downtown Chicago. Exiting the tollway meant paying a toll when you exit and paying again when you re-enter. There are, however, service plazas where one could stop for gas, or have lunch. Those plazas are built directly over the interstate. It's interesting to have lunch at McDonald's and watch the traffic fly past, directly beneath the plaza. It looked as if tall trucks were going to plow right into the floor beneath your feet.

Like New York and Los Angeles, Chicago is a city that never sleeps. The traffic became heavy as I got closer to O'Hare. From there, it was bumper to bumper all the way to Gary, Indiana where I turned south on interstate 65 toward Indianapolis. I sure was relieved when I saw the sign for Merrillville. Lots of motels and truck-stops there. I got a room at Super-8 and walked next door to Bob Evans family restaurant.

At eleven a.m. I was on the interstate 465 bypass on the northside of Indianapolis. I drove through the parking lot of the motel, but check-in time wasn't until three. I drove to the sports bar and they didn't open until twelve p.m. I just put the seat back for a short nap, but I couldn't fall asleep. There were just too many things to think about, so I picked up the book I was reading to pass the time.

Chuck Bixby was perhaps a few years older than me. And the way it sounded to me, he was a product of privilege. He grew up on the south shore of Lake Oneida, just north of Syracuse, New York. He graduated with a degree in business from Le Moyne college in Syracuse. I'm not sure how he ended up in Ohio working for Nacom. However, he had gone out of his way to learn the telecommunications industry. In the early 90s, he was running things for Nacom in Cincinnati and living in a very upscale neighborhood. I had met and worked for him in Columbus and Cincinnati. Nacom was extremely excited about this new contract and they would use only those they knew and trusted for first impressions.

I walked in to find Chuck already seated and dumping artificial sweetener into his tea. He stood up, shook my hand and said, "Man I've heard you've been hopping around all over the place."

I said, "Yeah, you could say that."

He said, "That's what you wanted wasn't it?"

I said, "Yeah, you could say that too."

Then he asked, "Any regrets?"

I said, "Don't we all have regrets?"

He said, "Man, I wish I could do what you're doing. To be that free would be wonderful."

I said, "It's not a perfect life, Chuck. Let's talk about this Primestar thing."

He said, "I have a warehouse rented just off interstate 70, ten miles east of the city. You'll pick up your work orders and material there each morning and turn in your work from the previous day. You don't even have to turn in an invoice, just keep a copy for your records. The installation is simple. You'll dig a hole three-feet deep with a post-hole digger. Add water and concrete mix. Make sure it's well mixed then pound a steel post into it. The dish will be mounted on the post. You'll then use some specialty tools to align the dish to the satellite in space. The tools consist of a meter, and inclinometer and some small metric wrenches. Two days training and you'll be ready to go."

What Chuck didn't tell me was that the area we were expected to cover stretched one hundred and fifty miles in every direction from Indianapolis. Chuck's brother, John, was my instructor and the next day we installed three dishes in Greenwood, just south of Indianapolis. It was a relatively simple thing and I told John I wouldn't need another day of training.

I did a double take the next morning, when I saw that my first job was seventy miles away in Lafayette. I found myself driving north on interstate 65, the same route I had traveled two days before. It was a day when cell phones were just beginning to become popular and we didn't miss what we had never had. Besides, they were still very expensive. When I got to Lafayette, I found a payphone and called the customers. Even though the two jobs had Lafayette postal addresses, they were very rural. My first stop was eight miles to the east of town and the next was eleven miles north-west of town. But driving didn't bother me, the weather was perfect and autumn in this part of the country was just beginning.

The next day, I was assigned work in the direction of Crawfordsville. Again, it was only postal addresses. I had to call each customer from a phone in town and write down lengthy directions in order to find where they lived. I drove for miles, as two-lane highways led to dirt roads, to long, washed-out lanes. However, once again, I considered it to be just another adventure. After a few days, I was becoming more proficient. The work seemed to be much easier and I was able to complete installations in a fraction of the time.

But what I missed was the comradery and kinship of working in groups. The only time I saw other installers was early in the morning when we met at the warehouse for supplies. Even then, everyone was in a hurry. There were four-hour time frames to meet and the earlier we got started the earlier we were done for the day. I must admit, I too was in a hurry, but not to be done for the day. That would only mean lonely hours in a motel room. Yet somehow, it was a loneliness I felt I needed.

I took my workload one day and headed west on interstate 70, then north on highway 231. I was on my way to a little place called, Greencastle. But once again, the jobs were located as much as fifteen miles outside of town. I was driving down a curvy dirt road when I saw three little children run from the road and hide behind some hedge bushes. They had left a plastic Halloween pumpkin in the road. I slowed to a crawl, I was afraid they would run back into the road for the pumpkin. When I got closer, I saw that the pumpkin was moving, so I stopped to investigate. The opening in the top of the pumpkin had been covered with duct tape, and inside was a tiny kitten. They were trapping it inside the pumpkin, placing it in the road to be flattened by passing cars.

I carried the poor thing in the direction of the closest house which was a mobile home on the other side of a creek. Just then, a middle-aged woman stepped onto the front porch and said, "What's up?"

I asked, "Are those your children?"

She said, "One's my daughter's and I'm babysitting the other two." I held out the kitten and the pumpkin and asked, "Didn't you see what they were doing?"

She threw up her hands and said, "I can't do anything with them."

I said, "Well if you're babysitting, then why don't you do your job?"

She said, "Why don't you mind your own f---ing business."

As I walked back to my truck, I yelled over my shoulder, "I suppose there's a reason they're not in school?" And you know? I still don't know why they weren't in school.

Once in a while I got work orders in Indianapolis, but I enjoyed those long, drives through the country. I didn't know until I picked up the work orders which direction I was going to be traveling. It was sometimes a hundred miles on the interstate until I exited for a long cross-country trek. It was a hidden blessing. I saw things I would never have the opportunity to see again. As folks continued to fly ahead on busy highways, I thought, *"Man you don't know what you're missing."* Indiana license plates in the early 90s, featured a twilight horizon with a silhouette of a farm, complete with house, barn and silo. The caption at the bottom read, 'Amber waves of grain'. It was perfect for Indiana. There were amber waves of grain, and much more.

I saw things that were new and unexpected. I had heard of the most popular sights in Indiana, but it was those hidden ones that thrilled me. I have always loved the changing seasons. It seems to me that people in the small towns and crossroads are those who have the greatest appreciation for the changing seasons. It was autumn and it was once again the Halloween season in Indiana. Western Indiana is a photographer's flower garden in the fall. Winding dirt roads cross winding creeks and rivers, where for more than a hundred years, covered bridges gave shelter to travelers. Where young boys while away summer afternoons with fishing poles, dreaming that one day, they would hook that legendary bass or catfish.

There are Amish folks living in Indiana. Signs warn caution that horses and buggies still share the road. And it's a warning best heeded. Law enforcement officials frown on anyone who fails to give the buggies their share of the road. Amish folks do things in ways of old tradition. They still drive to town in horse-drawn buggies. They still use horse-drawn plows and reapers. Harvests are still gathered in wagons and corn still stands in fodder shocks in the fields. It's like a step back in time. Much like what I had lived as a child, growing up in Kentucky. I will never forget those warm autumn days and those long country roads. There are scenes and sounds in my mind of lazy sunny afternoons. Even with the windows closed, I could hear the sound of the tires in the leaves.

Driving down dirt roads I glanced in the rear-view mirror to see the autumn leaves blowing and spinning just above the ground in the wake of my truck. Horses or cattle that were grazing along fences close to the road, galloping away in confusion. The feeling that it was I who disturbed the tranquility of that moment.

I think the most rewarding aspect of my work was the gratitude of the people. They had heard rich folks brag about all the wonderful shows they enjoy, with cable TV or satellite service. And now it was affordable, and the cable companies were even paying for the installation. They were amazed when I walked to various areas of the property, looking through the inclinometer to determine a line of sight for the dish. They watched as the hands on the meter began to register. Then when the LNB (Low Noise Block) was pointed directly at the satellite, the meter would emit a high-pitched buzzing sound.

At this point I had already attached a cable to the TV, but there was still no image on the screen. Then when I turned the set to channel three, a beautiful rose would appear in perfect digital clarity. That picture was a screen saver, and along with music, was the only thing the satellite would deliver until it was activated. The sound was also of perfect quality. I'll never forget the song. It was by Melissa Etheridge, *I'm The Only One*. And you know? I still like that song.

There was only one step remaining in the process. I would have to call a toll-free number from the customer's phone. It was the activation center in Philadelphia. The satellite receiving box, or converter would then make a sound like someone dialing an old rotary phone. When the call center answered I gave them my name, tech number and the serial number from the converter. Then suddenly the TV would become operable. A quick run through the channels to ensure they were getting the services they had ordered, and I was on my way.

Years of watching snowy channels and double images. Hundreds spent on rooftop or antennas mounted on towers and the same results. Poor reception and weather fade. Now, however, regardless of the quality of the TV, they could receive seventy-eight, perfect channels. Unimpeded by anything, perfect, digital quality directly from outer space to their TV. I had actually seen them jump for joy.

Chapter Eighteen

One of my favorite places to work was scenic Brown County. It was about sixty miles south of Indianapolis. It was hilly, one could almost say mountainous. It was not a place to be in a hurry. Roads were often steep, curvy and often without guard rails. There are lots of scenic overlooks and historic markers throughout Brown County. But the one I remember most was the day I happened upon the Story Inn in Nashville, Indiana. Built in 1851, the old inn still offers rooms for rent, and a delicious menu.

I had lunch, and as I walked back to my truck, I saw an historic marker near the road and I just had to investigate. A tarnished bronze plate was mounted on a moss-covered altar-like podium built of stone. A sign on a post next to the monument said, 'The 9:30 line'. The words on the plaque were tarnished but still legible. The podium stood on a site where a tall hickory tree had stood. It was nine thirty on the morning of September 9th, 1809. General Anthony Wayne and his entourage met with Tecumseh of the Shawnee and his entourage.

They made a treaty with the Shawnee that morning and the shadow of the hickory tree would be a deciding factor. The Indians were promised all lands to the west of the shadow of that tree. They were told to imagine that the shadow continued in a straight line to the west end of Lake Superior. They were told that if the sun were shining from the other direction, its shadow would point to Galveston Bay. They were told that from that day, no white people would encroach beyond the imaginary line. However, it was a loosely made and frivolous treaty, that was never intended to be honored.

I would like to share one more of my adventures in Indiana. I happened into a little town in western Indiana called Dana. There in front of a well-kept home was another historic marker. The sign read, 'Home of Ernie Pyle'. Born in 1900, Ernie Pyle was a journalist. He traveled the country telling stories of everyday people during the great depression. In 1940, he went to England to report on the Battle of Britain. When the United States joined the war, he reported from the frontlines, in north Africa, Sicily and France. He could have reported from the rear echelons, but Ernie chose to be up front with the boys. Soldiers called him, 'Our buddy'. He was then assigned to cover the war in the Pacific. It was there that he was killed by enemy fire on August 8th, 1945. Soldiers who knew him donated a plaque. It simply read, 'We thank you. Our Buddy'.

Autumn wore on and the phone rang in my room the week before Christmas. Chuck Bixby sounded excited, as he was full of humor, and inside jokes. I knew something was coming down the pipe. I said to him, "You know Chuck? You should go into politics. What's up?"

He said, "Oh busy, busy, busy. I called to see if you'll help train some guys in other areas. We just picked up the contract for Charleston, West Virginia. I would like you to spend a couple of weeks over there, then join us here in Cincinnati."

I said, "I don't mind, Chuck, but not till after the first of the year."

He said, "Fair enough, I'll let the guys over there know, to expect you the first week in January."

As I walked to my truck the next morning, I heard the phone in my room ring. I fumbled with my keys trying to unlock the door, but the caller had hung up before I got to the phone. I was sure it was Chuck, so I waited a few minutes and when the phone didn't ring, I went to work and thought no more about it. I had grown to love the people of Indiana and I knew I was going to miss them. They were always kind and hospitable, but the closer it got to Christmas the more kind they were. They almost treated me as if I were a victim, who shouldn't have to work at such a time of year. And even though there was snow on the ground, it wasn't very cold at all. Yet I heard comments such as, "Oh, you poor thing. You're going to do this work in the bitter cold?"

Christmas was the only day I didn't work during the holiday season. Two days after Christmas, the phone in my room rang. I picked it up and said, hello, but there was silence for a few seconds, and I was about to hang up when a soft feminine voice said, "Wynn, it's Cindy."

As you can imagine, I was confused. All I could say was, "UUUUH, Cindy! Good to hear from you. How on earth did you find me?"

She said, "I called the local office, and they gave me the number for the main office in Columbus. It's a long story. It took a little detective work, but I tracked you down."

I said, "OK, why?"

She said, "I can't explain it. There's just some profound reason I had to find you."

I said, "Well Cindy, I'm not exactly twenty miles away any more. It's a long way from here to the Twin Cities and I have no plans to go back there."

She said, "I know, but I'm coming to see you. My plane arrives at six this evening."

I said, "Now wait a minute, Cindy. That's just not a good idea. I'm busy and I'm running all over the place."

She said, "I don't care. I will run with you. Now are you going pick me up at the airport, or do I have to wing it?"

It was a day when you could park in short term parking, show your ID and walk all the way to the jetway. I was there to meet Cindy, and as we walked to baggage claim, she was talking a mile a minute. She was so excited to be there, and I was still trying to figure the whole thing out. Once again, she said, "There was just this profound reason I had to find you, and here I am. Aren't you proud of me? I mean, that I was able to track you down?"

I said, "Yes, Cindy, but I'm still wondering why. Your life is in Minnesota and mine is… everywhere."

She said, "But don't you want to settle down some day?"

I said, "Probably. But I'm not sure when or where. Right now, I'm happy with the life I'm living. How long are you going to be here?"

She said, "Two days, but it almost sounds like you don't want me here."

I said, "That's not it at all Cindy. It's just so unexpected. I'm scheduled to work, and I can't change that."

She said, "That's OK, I'll tag along, if that's all right."

We had fun those two days. Cindy interacted with the customers and was fascinated by their accent. The scenery was also new to her. I worked in Brown County those two days and she called it a wonderland. Those two days passed quickly, and my intention was to take her to the airport and put her out of my mind. I told her I was going to be going to Charleston, then to Cincinnati. She said, "Fine, I will see you in Cincinnati in about three weeks."

I said, "But Cindy. What about your career?"

She responded, "I can transfer to any city that has a Denny's. And Cincinnati does. I already checked. Trust me, I know what I'm doing."

I took Cindy to the airport on Friday, December 30th. The next day was New Year's Eve. I worked near Crawfordsville that day. And I have never before, nor since, seen fog so dense. I stood under an oak tree and I couldn't see the top of that tree. I was sure I wouldn't be able to get a satellite dish to work. I wasn't even sure if there were trees or hills blocking the line of sight. I installed two systems and I did them with nothing more than the instruments. To me, the picture on those TVs were grainy and snowy. However, both families were elated. I told them, "If you're happy with this reception, just wait till the fog clears."

I got to my room and called the front desk to see if I had missed any calls. The answer was no. I was sure Cindy would call any minute, but I waited for over two hours and the phone didn't ring. All the world was celebrating New Year's Eve. I took a shower and walked over to the sports bar. The rock group, The Eagles, had gotten back together. They had done a concert for HBO, and the bar was playing the concert on their large screen TVs. It was the *Hell Freezes Over* album. I had always liked The Eagles, so I sat in a back corner, drinking Bud Light until the concert ended about eleven thirty p.m., then walked back to the motel. The receptionist was at the front desk and once again I asked if I had missed any calls. Again, the answer no. I turned on the TV and watched the countdown and the ball drop at midnight, to end the year, 1994.

Chapter Nineteen

The next day was Sunday, New Year's Day. I ate cereal form a Styrofoam bowl for breakfast. Once again there was a *Twilight Zone* marathon on TV. I had seen every episode, but I watched them again and waited for the phone to ring. At dinner time I microwaved a TV dinner. The phone remained silent. I tossed and turned that night. I guess I had grown tired of lying in bed. I couldn't wait for morning, and when it came, I put my things into my truck and headed east on interstate 70.

I followed 70 to Dayton, Ohio and turned onto highway 35, east, to Chillicothe. From there I followed US 23, south, along the Scioto River toward Portsmouth. That was an all too familiar road. I had traveled that road in 1971, when I left home. When I got to Portsmouth, I turned east along the Ohio River toward Huntington, West Virginia. That area was even more familiar. I had worked that entire area when I was in the service. I was stationed in Ashland just on the other side of the river as a recruiter for the Marine Corps in 1979. Charleston would also be familiar. There was an active reserve center in Charleston, and I had to report to my commanding officer there once a week.

The recruiting office was in a small building on Winchester Avenue on the east side of Ashland. Recruiters from all four branches of the military worked there. The army, navy and Air Force never seemed to have any problems recruiting. Especially the Air Force and navy. They often had recruits waiting for them when they opened for business each day. There were three of us looking for potential marines and we struggled. Our quota was eight per month and we seldom made quota. We were allowed to search for recruits one hundred and twenty miles in three directions. However, there was a recruiting office in Huntington, West Virginia twelve miles away and we were not allowed to 'poach'. We were not to cross the Ohio River into Ohio or West Virginia. I had a tough time following that rule. I remember how angry the major would get when we failed to make quota.

We had to follow certain guidelines. We could accept two non-high school graduates per month if they could pass the written exam. There could be no criminal record. If there were minor offences, local judges would sometimes expunge criminal records to allow young men to start a career. I say young men, because there were very few women in the corps, in those days. I remember a young man, his name was Jamie Reeves. He wanted to be a marine more than anything in the world. However, Jamie had too much of a criminal record. The judge refused to expunge his record. He killed himself a short time later with a shotgun.

I remember some colorful characters. For me, it was hard to judge whether or not a kid had what it would take to be a Marine. My policy was recruit everyone I could and let the AFEES sort them out. AFEES, was Armed Forces Entering/Enlisting Station. I remember a young man, who in all appearance, just didn't have what it takes. Frankly, I thought he was just plain dumb. But to my surprise he passed all the tests. He came back to see us after bootcamp. He had been assigned to the air-wing's avionics. He would be working on jet aircraft.

When we were lucky enough to get a candidate, we took them to the AFEES, in Beckley, West Virginia for a physical examination. From there they were sent to basic training. Recruiters and recruits would arrive in Beckley the night before the physical and spend the night at the President Hotel. Sounds luxurious. It wasn't. It was probably the oldest building it downtown Beckley. The rooms were dark with small windows. The dark brown woodwork, had names and hopeless messages from draftees, dating back to the Korean War. It frightened some recruits. It was a preview of reality, of just how mean the outside world might be.

I remember two guys who had been buddies since first grade, and they had joined under the buddy program. Most guys (including them), thought this meant they would be together throughout their time in the corps. But the only guarantee was bootcamp. The two of them were, as they say, wishy-washy from the beginning, and one night in the President Hotel was the deal-killer. All was quiet until just after midnight when there was a knock at my door. I opened the door and there was the two of them and they looked to be scared out of their wits. They must've rehearsed, for they both spoke in unison.

"We're homesick. Is there any way that we can get out of this?"

I wasn't surprised. I said, "Tomorrow, you'll be given a medical history form to fill out. Just list something that you've had problems with. For instance, back pain, or even ongoing problems with athlete's foot."

The next day, I was waiting in the lobby of the AFEES, when a navy doctor called me to the counter. I asked, "What can I do for you lieutenant?"

He said, "Sergeant Johnson! Are you sure these two Joes want to go into the corps?"

I said, "I'm sure they don't. Why?"

He said, "Look at this medical form. They've marked every ailment that could be wrong with a human being. Now look at this side of the form. These are things that could only be wrong with a female. Take them home and tell them to stay there." He thought it was funny, but to me it was embarrassing and frustrating. That part of my life felt as if it had taken place in another dimension, even though it had only been sixteen years.

I thought it was ironic when I was handed work-orders for areas near Beckley, sixty miles south of

Charleston. The West Virginia turnpike runs south from Charleston and its now a freeway, interstate 77. The road was being built when I was hauling recruits to Beckley. Mountainsides were blasted away creating towering cliffs that had been stair-stepped to prevent landslides from pouring onto the highway. On steep, downhill grades, escape ramps were carved up onto the cliffs with large piles of sand to help stop runaway vehicles when brakes have failed. Blasting would occur early morning, and early afternoon. Sometimes traffic was stopped for as much as an hour until the roadway was cleared. The scenery is nothing short of spectacular, but the highways can be treacherous. Steep mountains tower above, as the Kanawha River snakes its way toward the Ohio deep in the canyon below. Once again, it was like a step back in time. Where did sixteen years go? And even more troubling, the years were passing faster each year.

The guys I trained in West Virginia were excited about learning a new trade. They were energetic and willing, therefore, they were easy to train. I trained them for two days and they were ready to go on their own. After the first two days, the work was to the west into Kentucky, or southern Ohio. Places such as Ironton, Ohio, Grayson, Olive Hill and Morehead, Kentucky. Even though, it was January, the temperature was somewhat moderate, but the sky was usually overcast. After two weeks I packed up and headed west on US 52 along the Ohio river toward Cincinnati.

The entire route is registered as a scenic byway and for good reason. Victorian era homes stood high on the hills where fields and pasture lands sloped downward to the river. Weathered barns that were built only a few generations after the Shawnee were forced from the area. Scenic overlooks and parks, each with their own historic tale. Places where men such as Daniel Boone and Simon Kenton led hunting parties in search of food for starving settlers. Ohio was the name given by the Iroquois, meaning, Good River. For thousands of years the area was ruled by native tribes and governed by such noble men as Logan, Cornstalk, and Tecumseh.

The afternoon rush hour was just getting under way when I got to the I-275 outer belt. Nacom's office was in the north-west area of the metro, so I went back to the same motel where I had stayed two years before in the suburb of Forest Park. That proved to be a good move as most of the work was to the south into Kentucky and west into Indiana.

I hadn't heard from Cindy since I took her to the airport in Indianapolis. As the days passed and became routine, I had almost stopped thinking about her. One night in the first week in February, the phone rang. Cindy had tracked me down again. She didn't even say hello, she just said, "Guess what, I'm coming to see you again."

I said, "For God's sake, Cindy. Why?"

She said, "I already told you. I want to be with you. Unless you don't want me. I'm flying in to the Cincinnati airport, which is in Kentucky. Is that right?"

I said, "Yes, the airport is in Florence Kentucky.

I picked her up on Sunday February 5th. I asked her how long she was going to be around, and she said, "Just a couple of days."

I said, "Well Cindy, I have to work, you know."

She said, "That's OK, I'll tag along."

I said, "You've got to quit this Cindy, before you drive us both crazy."

She said, "Well then, let's find an apartment and I'll move to Cincinnati."

I said, "Cindy, I don't even know how long I'm going to be here. Besides, you've never lived anywhere but Minnesota. All your friends and family are there. You're sure to get homesick."

She said, "That's just it. I've never been anywhere else. I want to experience the world too and you're the guy I want to see it with. Didn't Chuck say that you could have permanent work in Cincinnati?"

I said, "Yeah, but I've learned one thing in this business. If they promise you years, you can expect months, if they promise you months, you can expect weeks. The problem is I just don't know. And I don't know if I want a permanent location."

During the next two days she convinced me that we should live together. She went home to Minnesota to pack and I rented a two-bedroom apartment in Forest

Park. I flew to Minnesota and rented a moving truck from U-Haul and a trailer for her car. We put her things in the apartment, and I took the rented truck to London, Ohio to get the things I had stored there three years before. It was delightful having someone to come home to and it was strange not to be lonely.

On Valentine's Day I was working near Paris, Kentucky. I had never seen so many cats and dogs at one house. A single mother and her teenaged daughter had created a refuge for lost and homeless animals. The lady offered me a free kitten and I said, "No, I don't think so." But during the time I was there I noticed a black and white tuxedo kitten. It was running around with a pack of dogs as if it were a puppy. The dogs were carrying sticks, balls and other things in their mouths and so was the kitten. I said to the lady, "If the offer still stands, I'll take that black and white kitten."

She said, "Isn't he adorable? He thinks he's a dog. You can take him if you promise to give him a good home."

I said, "That kitten will never be cold or hungry again."

She said, "That's wonderful. Three young guys came by here and asked for full grown cats one day. I didn't question them. I let them have three that were almost full grown. They used them to train their hunting dogs. My daughter and I drove by their house and saw those dogs tearing the poor little things apart."

I said, "Not me, lady. I'm an animal lover."

Cindy was surprised when I gave him to her as a Valentine's Day present. She jumped for joy, clapped her hands and celebrated like a child. She named him Thor. I had stopped at Kmart for food, litter and a litter pan for him. And I also picked up a couple of toys. One was a rubber spider that would become his favorite toy. Thor would play fetch as long as someone would throw that spider. Every morning he would bring that toy and place it into my hand. The poor little thing was mute. The veterinarian said it must have been extreme cold that damaged his vocal cords.

Every day was an adventure. One day I was driving up a steep hill in Maysville, Kentucky when there was a violent pop and the truck stopped moving forward. I was no mechanic, but I knew the clutch had gone out of my truck. I called a tow truck and the driver said, "Old Bobby can fix her up." I climbed into the front seat with him and he took it to a place just a couple hundred yards away. It was a weathered, grey wooden building with no sign or any other indication that it was a repair shop. It was late on a Thursday, and 'Old Bobby' was drinking a Stroh's beer. Judging from the empty cans I'd say he had been drinking for a while.

He pointed and said, "Put it over there, I'll get to it in the morning." I told him I thought it was the clutch and he said, "I'll figure it out."

The tow truck driver charged me one hundred dollars. I paid him, but I thought he was overpriced. He offered to take me to the nearest motel, but the main part of town was just a half mile down the hill, and I told him I would walk. I found a room in an old historic hotel. I called Cindy to let her know I wouldn't be home. Then I called Nacom to let them know my truck was down. I didn't have a book to read, but I found a Bible in a drawer next to the bed and read from the Old Testament.

It had once been a luxury hotel, but now just a novelty for travelers who could say they had spent a night somewhere off the beaten path. The room featured an alcove with a view of main street and between buildings to the Ohio River. A new shopping center just outside of town did little to disguise Maysville's identity. It was an old river town, settled at a time when the river was the highway. Maysville was in the spotlight in 1980 when an earthquake hit the area. The epicenter was Maysville.

Until then few had known of the New Madrid fault which runs along the Ohio River. However, historians knew of the fault. It was said to have been one of Tecumseh's prophecies. He said to the then governor of the Northwest Territory, Ohio, Indiana and Michigan, William Henry Harrison, "I will go to Detroit. I will stamp my feet and buildings will crumble. I will make the rivers flow backward and leave their banks." It's still a mystery, but on the day that Tecumseh had predicted it, an earthquake occurred. Scientists believe, that if there had been a way of measuring it, the quake of December 11th, 1811, would have the most powerful ever to occur. Buildings did crumble and ripples on rivers caused by aftershocks created the illusion that rivers were running backward.

My brothers, Charles and Jimmy, were the best mechanics I knew, but they were more than two hundred miles away. I did call Charles to get his opinion on what I might expect for the repair bill. He said, "I doubt it's the clutch. Your truck is fairly new, but that's the worst-case scenario. That could cost you as much as five hundred dollars. But I think it's probably just a U-joint."

About three p.m. the next day, Old Bobby called me. He said, "Got-her-done." I walked to his shop and found that my truck was still inside. He said, "I always keep-um inside till I get paid."

I said, "Fair enough, how much is it?"

He said, "It's just over nine hundred dollars and I don't have one of them card things. You'll have to have to pay me in cash." He had scribbled some illegible marks on a sheet of notebook paper, but I could make out the total. Nine hundred and forty-nine dollars, and forty-nine cents. Then he added, "I won't take a check from you, I don't know you and you live all the way over in Cincinnati."

I said, "If you can't take a credit card, you're going to have to accept a check."

He just said, "Come back when you have cash."

I walked back to town and called the police. I didn't want the man arrested, I just needed a negotiator. Without going into details, I had come to the conclusion, the man was an idiot. A sheriff's deputy

175

picked me up and had little to say as we returned to the shop. Old Bobby turned a couple of different shades of red when we walked in.

The officer said, "Hello, Bobby. What would it take to resolve this mess?"

Old Bobby responded, "Cash."

The officer said, "I can see your concern, Bobby, but this guy's stuck here. Tell you what. I've got all his information. You accept his check and if it's bad, I'll go to Cincinnati, pick him up and throw his ass in jail myself."

Old Bobby said, "Well, Dave, I guess I'll have to take your word."

The deputy looked at me and said, "Do you agree with this deal?"

I said, "There's little more I can do. This son-of-a-bitch had already charged me double and he's holding me hostage for my vehicle."

He just said, "Take your truck and get out of here. That check better be good." When I got into the truck, I saw that there were spots of black grease in several places on the front seat. I tried to stop the officer to point it out to him, but he ignored me and drove away.

I made it home, and the next day, I drove to the little northern Kentucky town of Cynthiana. I had finished my first job, and when I pulled onto the main road, the problem occurred again. I called a tow truck and had the driver take me and the truck back to Old Bobby. We got there about mid-afternoon. Old Bobby said, "Park it over there out of the way and I'll look at it in a few days."

I asked the driver if he knew of someone else who could fix it. He said, "Let's take it to Terry and Joann."

It was about fifty miles from Cynthiana to Maysville and another five miles to Terry and Joann's shop. I felt better about leaving my truck with Terry and Joann. Terry was the mechanic and Joann took care of the books. Everything about them told me I was dealing with good and honest people. I told them about Old Bobby and a short version of the story. Neither of them said anything, but Terry gave me a look that said, 'I can't believe you trusted that guy'. Terry just said, "I'll get right on it and I'll call when I know something."

The shop was located to the rear of the property. Their home was about a hundred yards from the road. It was a post-World War Two style with a front porch and dormers that indicated a couple of rooms upstairs. There was a wooden patio at the back, facing the shop and woods beyond a small yard. Young walnut trees stood in the front yard. There was a circle of stones with an American flag on a flagstaff at the center.

This time, the tow bill was three hundred and twenty dollars. I called Cindy and she said, "Give me directions and I'll come and get you." She was there in less than two hours and I asked if she would take me to the courthouse. She said, "Sure but, why?"

I said, "Because I'm going to file a lawsuit against Old Bobby.

She laughed, clapped her hands and said, "This is just like in the movies. But honey, you know you'll never get justice in this little town. Everybody knows everybody. There's sure to be a good-old-boy network here."

The clerk gave me a form to fill out, with several lines to list the reason for the lawsuit. I wrote it out in detail. I was asking for one thousand dollars in damages, plus court costs even though that would not cover the repairs, towing and other expenses. I paid thirty-five dollars for the filing and an extra twenty-five dollars to have the summons delivered to Old Bobby by the sheriff's department.

Terry called me about mid-afternoon the next day and said the truck was ready. He was careful not to say anything bad about Old Bobby. He only told me what had to be done to fix the problem. He said, "Look I don't know who did the work, but someone put a new clutch in this vehicle. The problem is, they failed to resurface the flywheel, and overall, the work shoddy. It's a waste of time to replace a clutch if you don't resurface the flywheel. I had to do a lot to clean up what they did, but you deserve a break. Write me a check for three hundred and fifty dollars and we'll call it even." I drove that truck until later that summer, when I decided to buy a new one, but I never had another mechanical issue with it.

The next morning, I called and spoke to the editor of the *Cincinnati Enquirer*. He found the story of "Old Bobby" to be an interesting one. He also thought it would be in the best interest of the public to let them know that such a shady character was operating a business in their town. He told me to put the whole story on paper and he would print it. It was a full column' printed on the second page and was intitled, 'Beware of backyard mechanic'. I used the article to demonize Old Bobby, but I also exalted Terry and Joann for their help and understanding.

Finally, the day came to go to court. I got there early and took a seat in the back of the courtroom. A short time later, Old Bobby strolled in and took a seat near the entrance. I was a little nervous, but he acted as if court was something he did every day. Imagine my surprise when every single person who walked in seemed to know him. They all had the same greeting. "Hello, Bobbeh!" Lawyers in cheap suits with worn out briefcases.

"Hello, Bobbeh!" Then one of those cheap lawyers sat down beside him and I realized he had hired an attorney.

People appeared to go out of their way to walk past him and say, "Hello, Bobbeh!" We were asked to stand when the judge came in.

He said, "Please be seated. Hello, Bobbeh!"

I began to realize Cindy was probably right. This was not the place to expect justice. I think my case was the third to be called. I was directed to take the stand and Old Bobby's attorney opened a legal pad with a list of questions. He began with, "Why are you suing my client?" I told him and he said, "Did he refuse to redo the work when you took the truck back to him?"

I said, "No, he said he would look at in a few days. I told him I had to have my truck for work and transportation."

"So, you expected him to drop everything and work on your truck?"

I said, "That's right. I had paid him more than double the going rate for replacing a clutch, not to mention the towing bills, and other expenses."

He said, "How do you know what the going rate is for replacing a clutch?" I handed him a list of written quotes from other mechanics and a copy of the receipt from Terry Carter, the man who replaced the clutch. He said, "What kind of truck is it?"

I said, "It's a 1992, Ford F-150."

He asked, "How many miles are on it?"

I said, "At the time the work was done, it had just over fifty-eight-thousand miles."

He said, "Well, that ain't that old, not too many miles. Ever cross your mind that it could have been a factory flaw?"

I said, "No, it should have crossed his mind. He's the mechanic."

I was asked to step down and Old Bobby took the stand. I was allowed to ask him some questions, but I only had a couple. My first question was, "Have you ever had any formal training as an auto mechanic?" The answer was no. I asked, "Is it not protocol to resurface a flywheel before installing a new clutch?"

He said, "In the case of your truck, it wasn't necessary."

I said, "What if I told you that every one of the mechanics on this list told me it was absolutely necessary?"

I sat down and his attorney took over the questioning. He said, "Now, Bobby, I just have one question for you. Now I want you to tell the court Bobby. Ain't it true, you're studying to be a Baptist minister?"

I said, "I object, Christ was a carpenter, not an auto mechanic." The place erupted in laughter and the judge silenced everyone with his gavel.

Then he said, "I'll give you my decision in a few days."

I was quite proud of myself. I was glad to be done with court and I was sure I had won. As I walked past him, I couldn't resist saying, "So long, Bobbeh!" Three days later I got the judgement in the mail.

It said, "This court finds for the defendant. Plaintiff will make payment to Mr Bobby Caudill, in the amount of fifteen hundred dollars for damages and lost wages. Plaintiff will also pay court cost of one hundred dollars.

I was more angry than surprised. In fact, I can't tell the civilized world what I wrote on that paper before I returned it to them. I can tell you, that it did not contain one cent for Old Bobby, nor the court.

Chapter Twenty

I just realized that after all this time I have not described Cindy to the readers. Cindy was a pretty girl in so many ways. She was a buxom lady. She was about five foot five in height. She had long dark hair and the most piercing, dark eyes. She called herself, "A happy little heart." And I have to say that it was true. There was never a harsh word between Cindy and me. In fact, I don't recall that she ever raised her voice to anyone. I have to admit, I could never figure out what was going on inside her mind. There was something mystical about her. She was witty, intelligent and fun to be with. When she was asked a question, she would turn her head slightly to the right while maintaining a straight-ahead gaze through the corners of her eyes. She had never smoked and didn't drink. When she was younger, she danced in ballet competition. That ended with a skiing accident that crushed her left ankle. She had several surgeries to mend her foot and ankle. She walked without a limp, but she was never able to dance again. But Cindy loved to ski, and she refused to give it up. Cindy had no bad habits that I knew of. There was one thing about her that I found to be rather bizarre. She told me on several occasions, that she belonged to a group who practiced witchcraft. Some of the tales she told me were even more bizarre. The one I remember most was that the grand wizard cracked an egg into her open hand and the egg cooked before her eyes. You may choose whether or not to believe it, but she told me without a smile, or even a change of expression.

Seasons are evenly balanced in Ohio, especially southern Ohio. By the third week in March, robins were singing. The grass was green, hedge bushes had tiny leaves and were blooming bright yellow throughout the region. I'm not sure what those yellow blooming hedges are called, but my mother called them easter hedge. The Midwest is known for its cloudy weather from late October till spring. However, there are a lot more, sunny days in March, and even more as spring wears on. I had worked in some bitter cold conditions the previous winter and I was happy when spring arrived. Days were warm and sunny in March, there was more daylight hours and that made my work much easier.

There was a Denny's just two exits to the south on interstate 275. Cindy had no problem transferring her job from Minnesota to Cincinnati. She had worked for Denny's for more than ten years and she was very good at what she did. For that reason, the people in management were always willing to accommodate her. Cindy and I both cooked and we shared domestic chores equally. I had gotten used to having her with me and I looked forward to going home to her.

I was seldomly assigned work in the area. Much of it was west into Indiana, or south into Kentucky. Not far south of Cincinnati, horse country begins. It's beautiful country to visit, any time of the year, but spring and autumn are breath-taking. From small hobby farms to large corporate farms, boundaries are marked with board fencing. Perfectly painted white or pressure treated with black creosote, you'll seldom find a fence rotting or neglected. The same goes for houses and barns. Long driveways are fenced on each side and standing next to the fences are rows of catawba, or maple trees. Once again, I felt fortunate to have a job that I loved. And one that allowed me to get off the beaten path and see things that I would never have seen.

One day I came home from work and Cindy met me at the door with a concerned look on her face. She said, "Brian's been calling for you."

I said, "Blakely?"

She said, "Yep."

I said, "Where is he?"

She said, "Omaha. He sounds all excited. You know how he gets all worked up."

I said, "Did he leave a number?"

She said, "Yep."

I said, "OK, I'll give him a call tomorrow."

But before dinner was over the phone rang. Brian said, "Listen, you've got to come out here and help me out."

I said, "Brian I just got settled in here, I like it here and I like what I'm doing."

He said, "You know all those projects we talked about last spring? Well, they're happening. I have two major projects going. One for Cox Communications and one for US West Telephone. I've got more MDU work here than you could imagine. Lots and lots of overhead work. I've got a new bucket truck for you. I'll give you a salary in addition to your production pay, but you'll have to run the show. I have a crew of fourteen and Nacom is sending in some guys form the Denver office."

I said, "It's too much to think about tonight Brian. I'll call you tomorrow."

I told Cindy everything Brian had said, and she said, "I'm in it for the ride. I do like it here, but if it's a lot of work that will last, then maybe we should go for it."

I said, "I'm not crazy about moving to Nebraska. He's going to have to make some promises and some guarantees. Chuck's probably going to flip his lid."

She said, "I would like to give Denny's a couple weeks' notice."

I said, "In the meantime, I can go on out and find an apartment, then come back for you. We'll rent a moving truck and put your car on a trailer as before. This will put you a little closer to your family, Cindy. But it's also going to cost Nacom dearly."

I called Brian the next day and told him I could be there in two days. I told him my conditions, including a cellular phone which was very expensive in those days, but Nacom approved it. I told Brian he could have the task of breaking the news to Chuck. He said, "I already talked to him."

It was a repeat of two years before when I left for Minnesota. The difference is I had Cindy to worry about, but she seemed to be excited. I left on a Saturday, the first day of April. The route would be interstate 74 which runs north-west through Indiana and Illinois to Rock Island/Moline. I would stop there for the night, then take interstate 80 west through Iowa to Omaha.

It was spring in southern Ohio, but the further I drove north and west the more spring faded. By the time I got to Peoria, the fields were brown and there were few signs of spring. Again, I found myself second-guessing my decision. I promised to call Cindy when I got to Moline, so I turned on my new cellular phone and called my home phone in Cincinnati. I told Cindy I would be crossing the Mississippi River in a few minutes and asked her how she was doing. She said, "Oh, I'm a little lonely, a little scared. Just hope it all works out."

I said, "Yeah, I promise to do my best to make it work. I trust Brian and I think he'll be fair." I said goodnight and as I was crossing the Mississippi River it was eight p.m. and the sun was setting. A sign read, 'Fields of Dreams. The people of Iowa welcome you'. The first mile marker was 390. That meant that I was three hundred and ninety miles from the Missouri River, and Omaha.

It's called the Quad Cities. Rock Island and Moline are in Illinois, Bettendorf and Davenport are just across the river in Iowa. It was a busy area, but nothing compared to the rush and roar of Cincinnati. Even with the Sunday morning church traffic, there was a peacefulness about it. I had breakfast at a Perkins pancake house and got under way. In less than an hour, I was passing Iowa City. I couldn't believe it had only been a year since Brian and I were here creating bids for the veteran's hospital and the university. It all looked familiar, but it seemed so long ago.

The next landmark was Des Moines. Interstate 80 passes to the north of town. But there's one point where, if you happen to be looking south, a wide boulevard points directly into the capital building of Iowa. After Des Moines, it's about a hundred and thirty miles to Omaha and there's not much to see. Vast farms cover the land with few houses in sight. That was a testament to corporate farming. But there was a stark beauty, and as I have said, there was something peaceful about Iowa.

I got a room at a Comfort Inn on the west side of Omaha. It felt cold outside even though the sun was still shining. The next morning, the ground was covered with snow. I went to Nacom and Brian introduced me to his foreman, a man named Bill Perentie. I asked him how the work was going, and he said the crew from Denver kept putting things off. It was the rainy season and they were reluctant to work in the rain. I asked Bill to introduce me to the crew. We walked down a hallway and into the supply area. We found the crew lounging about smoking cigarettes and two of them were playing guitars. They were a motley looking bunch, dressed in ragged jeans, novelty T-shirts and tennis shoes.

Bill said, "Let me have your attention. This is Wynn Johnson. He's going to be in charge of things in the field."

I said, "We have a lot of work to get done and in order to do it there has to be rules."

Someone mumbled, "Here we go."

I said, "That's right. And here we go without you if you can't follow these rules. You're going to wear hard hats, steel-toed boots and decent jeans. I don't care what you wear for a shirt, because you're going to wear a reflective safety vest over it. Bad language and bad attitudes will not be tolerated. Two-way radios are to be turned on no later than six thirty a.m. You must be here by seven a.m. sharp. That gives us one hour to stock our trucks and get to the job site by eight a.m. Any questions?"

Someone said, "What if it's raining?"

I said, "What if it is? You get hungry when it rains don't you? Get yourself a poncho and pay no attention to the rain. Lightning is another matter. We will not climb the poles if there's lightning."

The same man said, "I'm not working in the rain."

I said, "No problem. You can go back to Colorado. The nature of our work is outdoors. If you can't work in adverse conditions, then you're in the wrong business. There are deadlines to meet and a lot at stake. Those are the rules. It's up to you."

I bought a newspaper and looked for apartments for rent. I found one in an apartment complex called Maple Hill Apartments. The building was located on a hill and the apartment was on the third floor facing west. Interstate 680 ran north and south at the base of the hill and beyond that was nothing but the great plains. There was a balcony and the view was astounding. But the interstate was only a couple hundred yards away and we'd have to get used to the noise of the traffic. I called Cindy and told her about the apartment. She said her last day at Denny's would be the 17th, I told her I would be there on the 18th, or the 19th.

I was shocked when every one of those guys were at Nacom's office the next morning. We loaded up what we needed and headed out to work in the rain. It was a much warmer day than it had been the day before, but the rain was steady. The guys wore wetsuits from a nearby sporting goods store. They wore work boots and hard hats with a Nacom logo on the front.

We were hanging three-quarter-inch cable to every apartment building with four dwellings or more. Attitudes were a little sluggish at first, but as the day passed, things began to change. They began to see that they could in fact work in the rain. They were delighted with the amount of progress and the amount of money they were making. They had been told that I was a hard-nose ex-marine infantry sergeant and they would learn to hate me from the beginning. And I was all the above. However, marine sergeants work alongside their troops and I began to earn their respect. I was just as wet, just as muddy and just as miserable as they were. I had true compassion for them, and they began to feel the same.

We worked long hours and long days. On a Friday afternoon one of the guys, Tyson Miller, came to me and said, "Wynn, I'm going to run to the convenience store for something to drink."

I said, "What time is it, Tyson?"

He said, "Almost three."

I said, "You know, I've heard that Goldberg's has the best tap beer and buffalo wings in town. Why don't we knock off early and go there for a beer?" We spent nearly four hours there and it was great for team building. Listening to their problems, hopes and dreams, I found them to be all American boys. I found a special kinship with them when I heard of their love for horses. We continued to work, and it continued to rain.

I told Brian the cost for airfare from Eppley Field in Omaha to Cincinnati and he let out a heavy sigh. I told him not to worry, I would take a bus for a fraction of the cost. I don't remember the exact time, but it was some ungodly hour of the morning long before daylight when I boarded the bus. It was Wednesday, April 19th,

1995. There were only a few passengers on the bus, and it was a quiet ride. I read for a while and I slept for a while. I had a two-hour layover in Chicago. It was a crowded and noisy place in downtown Chicago. I was ignoring the noise and completely immersed in the book I was reading when I looked up to see a special report on the TV. Someone had blown up a building in Oklahoma City, Oklahoma. Of course, we all know the history now. It was the bombing of the Alfred P Murrah federal building.

It was late when the bus rolled into downtown Cincinnati, but it was still daylight. Cindy was waiting for me at the bus station. We went directly to a U-Haul dealer and rented a moving truck. Cindy had already done most of packing, and by noon on the 20th, we were on our way. We stopped for the night in Danville, Illinois and completed the trip the next day. Cindy loved the apartment. We had our first night together in Omaha on Friday, April 21st 1995.

We spent the weekend getting settled in and on Sunday, we took a drive to explore the town. Thankfully, it was a sunny day. We had lunch at a small place in the historic section of downtown known as Old Market. Cindy appeared to be happy, but damn, I just couldn't figure her out. I drove her to a Denny's at the West Roads mall and she went in for an application. She came out, and as she got in, she said, "I can start on Wednesday."

When June rolled around, there were more sunny days and the weather was getting hot. By the end of June, the rain had stopped, and in just a few days, the ground was hard, and the grass was dry. There was an image of a chimney rock formation on the Nebraska license plate. I thought that if it were important enough to display on every car registered in Nebraska, I thought it would be worth seeing. I asked Cindy if she would like to take a road trip during the Fourth of July break.

The holiday was on a Tuesday, so we had four days off. We left on Saturday morning. We stopped for the night in Ogallala. We checked into a motel and went out to see what we could find for entertainment. Ogallala was known as, 'The town at the end of the trail'. Cattle driven from Texas was loaded on east-bound trains at Ogallala. Most notably, was John T Lytle who drove thirty-five hundred head of longhorn cattle from southern Texas. The drive inspired the novel, *Lonesome Dove*. We visited Boot Hill cemetery. An historic sign boasted of the wild-west days in Ogallala. There were twenty-one saloons in town. Cowboys would start at one end of town and attempt to drink a shot of liquor at every saloon until they reached the other end. The sign said that as many as three cowboys in one night fell victim to the town marshal's gun. There was a drive-in movie theater just outside of town. We saw a movie there called, *Seven*. It featured Morgan Freeman as a detective and Kevin Spacy as a serial killer.

The next day we headed north-west on the scenic by-way 26, along the Platte River. Long before there were highways, this had been the Oregon Trail. Scotts Bluff is near the border of Wyoming and the chimney rock was just a few miles further in the Polecat mountains. I had seen the chimney rock many times in the movies but being there is hard to describe. This too, looked to have been a playground for the gods. A perfect, round mound heaped evenly to a point in the center where a monolith towered above.

There was a parking area and a path leading toward the base of the mountain. Next to the parking area was a cemetery. The cemetery was created during the days of the covered wagon. The Oregon Trail ran past this spot in the long trek to Oregon. The bodies of those who died on the trail were buried in stages. For instance, if someone died after the wagon train left Omaha, the body was held until they reached Grand Island. The next burial site was North Platte, then Ogallala, then Scotts Bluff and so on. There's something sad and haunting about the graveyards along the Oregon Trail.

Looking from the parking area, the path looked to be straight and level. The ground was blanketed dark green with what looked to be prairie brush. But the path was not straight nor level. There were turns, gullies and the prairie brush, was about fifteen feet high, and the path was a tunnel through it. The mountain looked to be much closer than it was. My guess was about three quarters of a mile.

It was late when we reached the slope. It was a steep and rocky climb and Cindy waited for me near the base of the slope. When I finally reached the monolith, I realized I could go no further without professional climbing gear. I paused for a minute to watch the sunset, then headed back down. We started walking back when we heard a pack of coyotes somewhere in the distance. It was now dusk. I remember my exact words, "Isn't that neat?" A little further on, we heard the coyotes again. This time they were a lot louder and a lot closer. That's when we realized they were coming right down that path from behind us.

There is some history of coyotes being aggressive with humans, but not much. But they were wild animals and that could mean unpredictable. We ran as fast as we could to the truck, and we were gone.

On the way home, Cindy announced that she was going to drive to Minnesota the following weekend to see her family. She left on a Friday after work and I never saw her again. She called me a few days later. She was crying, she told me how much she loved me, but she just couldn't live in Nebraska. She begged me to move to Minnesota, but I felt betrayed. I told her it was out of the question. She said she had enlisted the help of her father and brother-in-law to help her move her things. She wanted to see me to say goodbye. I told her it would be too painful. I came home a few days later and her things were gone.

Cindy called me every night for the first month or so, until I convinced her I was not moving back to Minnesota. But Cindy always had a way of finding me. If I got a different phone number, she would somehow find it. In 2014, I joined the rest of the world and created a Facebook page. A few months later, Cindy found me. We messaged back and forth a few times, but then she died of cancer in the summer of 2015. She was only forty-nine.

Chapter Twenty-One

Omaha was never good for me after Cindy left. A broken heart can put all manner of thoughts into one's mind. "*What did I do wrong? It had to be my fault. There must be something wrong with me.*" But what I remember thinking most often was, "*This is karma. The gods are punishing me for something I did in another life, or something.*" All I know is that it was powerful enough to make me want to crawl into a hole for a while.

My eighteen-year-old son had graduated high school the end of May. He decided to take a break from school and live with his old dad for a while. I welcomed his company, but I did not approve of his break from school. He did eventually finish school to become an engineer. He also lived with me in Omaha for several months. He made friends quickly in Nebraska. He bought himself a new truck and I seldom saw him. He had concern for old dad, but he had his own problems. He had a tumultuous relationship with a childhood sweetheart in Ohio, who in my opinion, treated him poorly. She would dump him, and he would go away and start a new life. But then she would start calling him on the phone and he would abandon everything and run back to her. Just when I would get used to him being around, I would come home to find his room empty and his truck gone.

Work was my only relief from the loneliness of Omaha. Everyone around me had their lives and their families. It was much like Minnesota. I would come home from work to a silent, empty apartment. Yet there was life in that building. People had parties, cooked on the barbeque grill, or played with their children in the courtyard. However, there was no life in my apartment except for the little that was left in me. Nature has some strange ways about it. Just when you're ready to say, this is it, I can't take it anymore, another door appears. A change happens that is so different, so bizarre that your mind and your way of thinking are completely altered.

I remember one long Sunday. I went for a drive and had breakfast at Perkins. There was just nothing left to do but go to my apartment and do nothing. I took a book, a beer and some cashews and went out to the balcony to pass the time. The afternoon sun was reflecting off the building driving the temperature even higher. But the view made it all worth it. Once again, I felt I deserved to suffer, to atone for whatever I had done to offend the gods.

I looked up from the book, and there was a half-grown squirrel on the railing. I dropped a cashew at my feet. He jumped down, took it, then jumped back on the railing where he ate it. He sat there looking at me as if he wanted more. I dropped another cashew at my feet, and he jumped down for it but this time he ate it at my feet. The next one he took from my fingers. All my troubles were forgotten as I watched my new little friend. I named him Tex, and when his stomach was full, he too left me.

But the following afternoon he came back. I fed him from my fingers, he even hopped up on my knee. I talked to him, I even animated what he might be saying back to me. One afternoon I had just sat down, when I realized I had forgotten his cashews, but I hadn't seen him yet anyway. I went inside to get them from the cabinet, I looked down and he was at my feet. I put some cashews on the kitchen floor and left him there eating. I had spent hours playing with Thor. But Cindy took him when she left, leaving yet another void in my life. It was as if nature had sent this tiny little creature to help fill the void.

I watched him grow strong and healthy until he was full grown. But work began to keep me away from home a lot and I missed spending time with that little squirrel. It was a blisteringly hot and dry summer. Snow in the spring, torrential rain and then unbearable heat. I had not expected the extremes and it added to my depression.

You see, we were working on two very large projects. One was for Cox Communications, the other was for US West Telephone. Those two large corporations were in competition and fighting for a customer base in Omaha. We were rebuilding the system for Cox who were offering the best in cable TV entertainment. We were also building the world's first fully interactive cable TV system for US West. It was video on demand and it was called Telechoice.

Denver based US West sent two men to Omaha to put together a team to get the work done. They were Don Larson and Jack Langle. Those two were good managers administratively, but they had no hands-on experience. Their greatest concern was how to get apartment buildings wired for service. Brian and I met with them at several locations and I explained how we had done this in other cities. Nacom had two entirely different crews. One for US West, the other for Cox. My crew was working for Cox. Langle and Larson didn't know that. They thought I would be the one to lead their project.

It was midsummer 1995, when US West began to offer service. That's when they found out that I was not going to be working for their interest and they were furious with Nacom. I told Brian I would switch over to the US West crew, but then Cox got wind of this, and they too, were furious. Brian said he preferred that I stay with the Cox project.

I got a call from a man by the name Tim Terry. He was a field foreman for US West. He said he was representing his company and asked if I could meet him at Perkins the next morning for breakfast. I spent the rest of that day and most of the night wondering what it was all about. He didn't waste a lot of time. He said, "I'm here to speak for Jack Langle and Don Larson."

I said, "Is there some reason they couldn't speak for themselves?"

He said, "Yeah, you know, possible conflict of interest with the higher-ups."

I said, "OK. What can I do for you?"

He said, "Well, what do you need Nacom for? Why can't you do this work directly for us versus through Nacom? You know, cut out the middle man."

I said, "Well Tim, I have friends at Nacom, and Brian Blakeley is a very close friend."

He said, "We'll have to know very, very soon."

I called Brian and asked him to join me for lunch. There wasn't a lot of small talk, but I did say to him, "Brian. Why did we leave Minnesota for a place where the temperature is over a hundred degrees every day of the summer? Did you know that the temperature in the Twin Cities never went above ninety last summer?"

He said, "Just wait, the winters are just as extreme."

I started to tell him, and he said, "I've already heard about it. You know Nacom would hate to lose you, but as a businessman you know what I would do. By the way, do you know a guy by the name, Mark Olson?"

I said, "Yes, I know him. He works for King Video in the Twin Cities."

He said, "Well he doesn't work there anymore, and he's been calling the office looking for you."

I said, "Well, what does he want?"

He said, "I don't know. Bill Perentie took the call. You know I would be excited about this opportunity if I were you."

I said, "Yeah, but these big companies want to take forever to pay an invoice and I don't know if I could float a payroll for that long."

He said, "It's all up to you, my friend. You're going to have to figure it out."

I talked to Bill Perentie the next day. He told me that Mark Olson was now manager for a large cable TV company in Sioux City Iowa. The company was owned by *The Washington Post* and *Newsweek Magazine*. I called Mark from Bill's office. Olson said he remembered me from the Twin Cities. He asked if I would be interested in bringing in a crew to do a massive outside plant alteration. He went on to say that sixteen thousand electronic devices had to be replaced. I told him I would give it some thought.

Bill Perentie was beside himself with excitement. He said, "Hey man, this is huge. Let's start our own thing. Listen I've heard nothing but good things about you, Wynn."

I said, "No offence, Bill, but I haven't heard anything about you, good nor bad. I just wouldn't be able to fund an operation that size."

He said, "We only have to hold out for a little while, till the money starts coming in. Do you know Terry Lions?"

I said, "I know of him, he's the guy from Minnesota, right?"

He said, "Yeah, that's right. Well, he heard about you and US West. He's got some money and between the three of us this thing could be huge. In two years, it could be bigger than Nacom."

I'm going to shorten this part of the story as much as possible. I met with Bill Perentie and Terry Lions at a place called The Philadelphia just south-west of Omaha in Millard Nebraska. We made a verbal agreement to form a three-way partnership with equal say, equal pay for the three of us. I signed the contract with US West the next day. I then drove to Sioux City where I met with Mark Olson and his field foreman, Bruce Rosenfeldt. Those two were the kindest, most easy-going men I had ever met. I signed the contract and agreed to have a crew working the following week.

The new company was a disaster from the beginning. What I didn't know about my new partners was that one had a drug addiction. The other was taking antidepressants for paranoid schizophrenia. I was training a crew in Sioux City, while the other two were setting up the business in Omaha. In order to open a business account, I would have to stop in and sign the articles of incorporation at the bank. I signed in haste and failed to see that Bill Perentie had made himself fifty-one percent owner of the business. That gave him complete control.

Things were going well, and the money began to come in. I was in Sioux City when Bill called me and said, "Come and get your truck."

I said, "What are you talking about? I'm driving my truck."

He said, "Well, image is everything for a company. We now have matching trucks."

I drove to Omaha in a fury. There in front of the townhome where Bill lived were three brand-new 1995, Ford F-150s. Two of which were identical. Those belonged to Terry and Me. Bill had purchased for himself a top-of-the-line F150, with all the bells and whistles.

We had our first business disagreement. But I was still unaware that Bill had placed himself in total control of our company. I gave in after blowing my top for a couple of hours and started driving my new truck. About two weeks later, there was another new truck parked in front of Bill's place. That one was a brand-new Ford Ranger, with all the bells and whistles. Bill explained that the Ranger was for his girlfriend and that she would need it to deliver supplies to people in the field. I would have none of it. I demanded that the truck be returned the next day and Bill said OK.

And what a day that next day turned out to be. Terry was running an installation crew at an apartment complex called Fox Hill. He was having some problems with the project and asked if I would stop by and give him some instructions. The temperature was well over a hundred when I arrived at Fox Hill. Except for Terry, the entire crew was standing outside the building and an ambulance came ripping in. I asked the crew what was going on and one of them said, "It's Terry, man. He's freaking out."

I could hear him screaming from somewhere inside the building. I started in and a paramedic said, "Stay out here all of you."

They hauled Terry out on a gurney screaming with every breath, his hands over his face. Every now and then he would say, "You got to help me." The paramedics kept asking him where he was hurting. He finally said he was having a reaction to some drug he had taken. They asked him what kind of drug and he said, "Prozac." They asked him how many pills he took and at what time. He said, "One pill and at eight a.m."

The paramedic said, "Well it's one p.m. If the drug was going to cause a reaction, it would have happened before now."

The medics talked to him for about an hour and told him he should speak to someone about his depression. That's how I learned of his problems. I couldn't talk to him after that. I was afraid of saying something that would cause him another breakdown. I put Tyson in charge of Terry's crew and went back to Sioux City.

It was a hundred miles from Omaha to Sioux City. I was spending a lot of time driving back and forth putting out fires between the two cities. It was the middle of August when we started in Sioux City and the weather was very hot. I was shocked when in mid-September my son called me on the two-way radio from two poles away. He said, "Dad! Look around you. It's snowing. Summer had turned to fall that day, right before our eyes. My son, Jeremy, came and went like the wind. We drove back to Omaha that evening and he turned east on interstate 80 and kept going. I knew he was headed back to Ohio.

The next day was Saturday. I worked in Omaha until about two p.m. and headed home. I took a book, cashews and a beer and went out to look for Tex and watch the sunset. There was an ash tree just to the left of the balcony. The angle of the sun had shifted to the south and the tree was now blocking my view of the sunset. But that wouldn't be a problem for long, the leaves on that tree were yellow and falling.

Perhaps it was intuition, but something told me to run by Bill Perentie's place. There were three vehicles parked in front of his place, including the new Ford Ranger that he promised to return. It was Sunday afternoon so I would wait until Monday, but I was steaming mad. Terry was unable to function, and Bill was doing nothing to help with production. To make things worse he was living a lavish life and creating debt faster than I could make money to pay it. On Monday, Bill informed me that the Ford Ranger had over two thousand miles on it and couldn't be returned. I demanded that the truck be returned and that he pay for the damages. Then I went back to Sioux City.

Once again, I had a feeling that I was in a bad situation with my new business partners. I drove back down to Omaha and went straight to Bill's place. The blue Ford Ranger was gone and so was Bill's truck. There were overflowing garbage containers next to the driveway and all the drapes were closed. There was plenty of evidence that they had moved out and gone to who knows where. I called Bill's cell phone and there was no answer. I called the Ford dealership and the Ford Ranger had not been returned. I called the bank and the business account had been emptied. And it got worse. We had purchased an expensive computer, fax machine, copier and other office equipment. Bill had possession of all of it. My greatest fears had just come true.

Chapter Twenty-Two

I called Terry and all he could say was, "I told you so." Funny, I don't remember him telling me anything. I continued calling Bill, and after three days, he answered. After the shock of the sound of my voice, he stuttered and stammered, then told me he was in Des Moines. It gave me some hope at first when he told me he was there to bid for a massive cable construction project. But it only it only took seconds for reality to set in. I knew he was lying. And I somehow knew that if he was telling me he had gone east to Des Moines, he probably went west.

I called the police and spoke with an investigator. He told me there was little he could do. We had allowed Bill to own our company. My next fear was that Bill would change his phone number. He had more than thirty thousand dollars and brand-new vehicles. He could go anywhere he wanted, and in the eyes of the law, he had done nothing wrong. He had taken everything, and he had done nothing to earn it.

I spoke to everyone who knew him, and no one had any clues as to which direction he and his girlfriend had gone. I did learn that another Nacom employee had gone with him. His name was Brian Perentie. He was Bill's brother and the father of Bill's girlfriend's infant child. At the time, all I could do was pretend to believe Bill. I talked excitedly about joining him in Des Moines and how happy I was that he had found such a lucrative project.

I was now desperate. I went over to Bill's abandoned townhome to look for clues. All the while contemplating what I would do to him when I found him. I went to the back patio door and shook it violently causing the stick that was meant to hold it shut to fall to the floor. I went in to find what they had left behind. All the furniture was gone, but there was plenty for the property owner to have to clean up or haul away. Bags of clothing, empty boxes and children's toys. I never thought I would be so lucky. In a black plastic bag filled with garbage was a phone number and the name, Barb.

I rushed out to my truck and called the number. It was a lady in Lake Odessa, Michigan. I told her who I was, and she began to tell me everything I needed to know. She said that she was Brenda's mother. Brenda was Bill's girlfriend. She told me that both Bill and his brother, Brian, were drug addicts and that she feared for the life of Brenda and the baby. She said, both men were physically abusive. She said, "I want you to find them and bring my daughter and her baby home." Then she gave me an address in the Phoenix, Arizona suburb of Chandler. A few hours later, Terry and I were on a plane bound for Phoenix. We got a cab at the airport and I asked the driver to take us to the police station in

Chandler. I gave the desk clerk a short version of the story and she told us to have a seat. A man with a badge came out and introduced himself as detective Joe Parks. I still don't know why, but he believed our story. After telling us both how stupid we were, he said, "You gave this guy full legal right to take this stuff. The only thing I am willing to do is try to scare him into giving back what's yours. I'll have a couple of officers go along, but we will not go into that house or garage. If he resists, then there's nothing we can do."

The detective was kind enough to let us ride in the back seat of his car, and two officers followed in a squad car. I saw the trucks in the driveway and called Bill on my cell phone. He tried to sound excited, he said, "Wynn! When are you coming over to join me?"

I said, "I have come over, Bill. Look out your window." The three officers got out and stood next to their cars facing the house.

Bill said, "OK, what do I have to do?"

I said, "Nothing. We just want what's ours." With that we walked into the house and started carrying out tools and computers. I said to Brenda, "Your mother asked me to bring you home. If you want to go, then put your things in the back seat of that white truck. Either way, I want you to use my phone and call your mother to let her know what you've decided to do."

She talked to her mother for ten minutes or so. She handed me back the phone and said with a helpless look, "I guess I'll stay here."

I said, "Fine, Brenda. Where's the money?"

She said, "Bill and Brian stopped at casinos along the way. I don't think there's any left."

I was a formidable foe in those days. I told Bill he'd better cough up some money. He gave me eighteen, one hundred dollar bills and swore he didn't have any more. I found Brian Perentie sitting by an upstairs window with a rifle across his lap. He said, "Wynn, I see Terry outside looking through the toolbox on my truck. He'd better not take anything that belongs to me."

I said, "You know, Brian? We could take everything you maggots have here and still not get back what you've stolen. And if you don't want that rifle stuffed somewhere you really don't want it, you'd better sit there and be quiet."

Terry didn't feel comfortable driving, so we went to U-Haul and loaded the Ranger onto a trailer. I guess it was a good idea, he was asleep twenty minutes after we got under way. Chandler is on the south side of the Phoenix metro and I needed to go north. I made my way through the city during the heart of the rush hour. I got onto interstate 17 and headed north. The first sign I noticed read, 'Flagstaff 125 miles'. That is where I would turn east on interstate 40.

The sun had gone down when I passed that sign. I was sure I could get to Flagstaff in two hours. Phoenix is in a bowl, or basin. I knew there would be some uphill driving, but I swear to you that drive from Phoenix to flagstaff is uphill all the way. Good thing the truck was new. Pulling the other truck on a trailer was a chore. I would use all the RPMs and horsepower the truck had to reach sixty miles per hour, then a curve or steep grade would slow me down to forty again. That leg of the journey took more than three hours. I stopped for gas at Flagstaff and Terry went inside to use the restroom. He came back with snacks, he devoured them and went back to sleep. I thought that after the uphill driving, it would be downhill for a while. But no. It was just a long level drive across the high plains. The first sign said, 'Albuquerque 320 miles'. I passed an exit for Meteor Crater Natural Landmark. The night was dark, but the stars were beautiful. Now and then I could feel a gust of wind blowing in from the north pushing the truck slightly to the right. It was the last week in October.

I turned on the radio and Terry complained. I turned it down, but I didn't turn it off. It was a soft rock station in Winslow. I listened until the station began to fade, then I found a country station broadcasting out of Holbrook. When I passed Petrified Forest National Park east of Holbrook that station too began to fade. I couldn't find a station after that, I just turned off the radio and listened to Terry's snoring. Must've been the drugs, I don't know another way that a person could sleep so much.

I was pleased when I passed a sign that read, 'Welcome to New Mexico'. I stopped for gas twenty miles or so east of Gallup. It was like something from the roadrunner cartoon. A small gas station stood at the base of a towering monolith. There were no other houses to be seen and there was only one gas pump in front of the station. It did, however, have a Subway restaurant inside. I remember saying to Terry, "You know? If they ever get to Mars, they'll probably find a Subway restaurant."

Terry was going out of his way to anger me. He was six foot four and boasted of having been a golden glove boxer in college. I don't know about that, but I can tell you he was as dumb as a mule. Look the man in the face and ask him a question and his face would go blank like the lights of a city going out. He was six or seven years younger and he thought that gave him the means to intimidate me. When he got in the truck, he slammed the door. When that didn't get my attention, he made all the noise he could as he ate his food, then he belched. I said, "Are you trying to say something Terry?"

He said, "Yeah, this is every bit your fault."

I said "I know. I picked a couple of dumbasses for business partners."

At that point he told me what he was going to do to me. I was just about to get on the interstate ramp. I slammed on the brake, and we both jumped out. I met him at a dead run and when I was just a few feet from him he threw up his hands and said, "I don't want to fight."

I said, "Then you get back in that truck and don't you open your mouth again."

He started walking away into the desert yelling, "I'll walk back to Nebraska."

I said, "You damn sure will if you don't get back in this truck. And you don't even have a heartbeat to think about it." I put the truck in gear and started rolling forward and he came running back. I don't remember hearing another word out of him.

The interstate continued level or with gently rolling hills. Then I was surprised to see a sign warning of a steep grade and warning truckers to use lower gears. Then there was a sign for a roadside rest and scenic overlook. I pulled into the site to stretch my legs and get some fresh air. There in the valley far below was the entire city of Albuquerque. All that uphill driving from Phoenix to Flagstaff, well it was time to leave the high plains at least for now. It's one of the most spectacular sights you'll ever see. A glimmering jewel hanging from the neck of the Rocky Mountains.

I had planned to get a room in Albuquerque, but it was three a.m. I put the seat back to nap in the truck. I was awakened by the loud popping of a trucker, engine braking to slow down for the grade. It was a crisp autumn morning and the sun was bright. I got out for some fresh air and take another look at the city below. Throughout the city, there were all the colors of an eastern city. Varieties of trees had been brought in, over the years. To the left and up the slope of a mountain were the indigenous bright yellow aspen and the dark green pine. Above the mountains was a dark, blue sky.

The thought that went through my mind was, *"Would make a great photograph for a calendar, or a jigsaw puzzle."*

Then all serenity left me, as I thought of the difficult situation I was in. I sat down at a picnic table to reflect before getting under way. I had two contracts that some contractors would kill for. The company we had formed was worthless as far as I was concerned. But the contracts were priceless, with good crews and management. Suddenly, an idea occurred to me. I had met some people in Florida who just might have an interest in my contracts.

It was a day when you got a different phone number every time you got a new phone or provider. There was a slim chance that the number would be the same. I took out my wallet and found a small, worn and folded piece of paper with the name Ronnie Barnes and a phone number. Barnes was general manager for a large cable TV installation company called Vir-Tech, based out of Jacksonville Florida. Even though the company's corporate office was in Florida, Barnes lived in the Washington DC area. It was ten after eight mountain time, so it was after ten in the east. I just had to know if the number was still good.

I called the number and he answered. I gave him a short version of the situation and he sounded excited. He said, "Call me when you get home." I got in the truck and began to formulate a plan. Vir-Tech would pay our company's outstanding debts. In return they would receive the rights to the contracts, outstanding accounts receivable and all assets including four new pickup trucks. As for me I would be happy just to walk away.

I didn't share my plan with Terry. Frankly I didn't care a hoot for his opinion. I made a quick stop for gas and refreshments in Albuquerque then headed north on interstate 25. There were some towns along the way, including New Mexico's capital city of Santa Fe. Next, would be, Pueblo, Colorado, Colorado Springs then Denver, where I would turn east on interstate 76. Looked simple enough, but it was four hundred and fifty miles from Albuquerque to Denver. And looking at the map, it looked like mountainous driving all the way.

It was a tough drive, but invigorated by my new escape plan and the scenery made it all worth it. Easy to see how the mountains got their name. There's a closer view of the mountains from Colorado Springs to Denver. Colorado Springs has all the makings of an old mining town, but to my knowledge, neither gold nor silver were ever discovered there. North of town the central plains lay to the east. Looking west the mountains appear to rise higher and higher. The dark green pine and the yellow aspen forest ends abruptly where the altitude becomes too high for them to grow. At that point, nature has swept away the soil to the gray granite cliffs just below the snow-capped peaks. In the canyon below, the white water rapids of Silver Creek sparkled in the sunlight. No question about it, the steep mountain drive is worth it.

The sun was going down when I got clear of the Denver metro. I was on interstate 76, but it was still more than five hundred miles to Omaha. Terry yawned and asked, "When are we going to be back in Nebraska?"

I just said, "Shut up, Terry."

It was about ten p.m. when I stopped for gas in Ogallala, Nebraska. Things began to look familiar as Cindy and I had been here a few months before. But it was not the bright, happy days of summer. I passed North Platte where Cindy and I had stopped for lunch at MacDonald's. I had only known her for just over two years, but I guess I would be thinking about her for a long time to come. Most of the fields had been harvested, like the words of the song, 'Dark flat land'. Terry grumbled, but I listened to the radio anyway. I was exhausted, but I had no intention of stopping.

It was four thirty a.m., when I parked in front of my apartment building. Terry woke up and asked, "Are we home?"

I said, "I am, but you're not."

He asked in a whining voice, "What am I supposed to do?" I handed him the keys and told him to unhook the trailer and drive home. But I had to help unhook the trailer. I guess it sounds insensitive, but he was everything I hate in a human. He was just plain lazy to the point of helplessness.

Ronnie Barnes arrived on Thursday, November 2nd. He and his company thought my offer was more than generous. When the deal was complete, he said to me, "What do you intend to do?"

I said, "Walk away, just like I said I would."

He said, "Now I have an offer for you. How about staying on here as our manager. We're going to rent an office and a warehouse. We'll advertise for help in Iowa and Nebraska. You can choose one of these trucks for a company vehicle. We'll pay for your gas for business trips. We'll give you a salary, production incentives and a signing bonus. Anything that takes place in Iowa and Nebraska will be your baby." I was very reluctant to stay in Nebraska, but I agreed to stay. At least for a time.

Chapter Twenty-Three

Terry packed up and moved back to Minnesota and I never saw nor heard from him again. I almost envied Terry. He was free from all the things that had dogged me for the past two months. I was beginning to realize that I too was missing Minnesota. I had enjoyed my stay in Minnesota. Only a year before I was in Indiana and I enjoyed that as well. Just about all the things that could haunt someone had cursed me in Nebraska. If not for those things, I'm sure I would have been as happy there as anywhere else. All this had given me mixed emotions about the decision I had just made to stay in Nebraska.

I had asked my son to come to Nebraska and help me with getting the crews under way again. He was there in two days. It was Sunday, November 5th, and it was time to check on things in Sioux City. I had always taken interstate 29 on my trips to and from Sioux City, but on that day, I decided to take scenic highway 75, north along the west bank of the Missouri River.

If anyone had ever done a study, they would probably find that more suicides occur on lonely Sunday afternoons than any other day of the week. And this was one of those days. To make bad matters worse, it was the day we turned back the clocks to end daylight savings time. The sundown would now be around five p.m. My son, Jeremy, decided to leave his truck in Omaha and ride along with me to Sioux City. From the time he was a little boy he had always tried to convince me to slow down, and as they say, "Smell the roses."

It was mid-afternoon and the sun was bright when we left Omaha. I was driving, so Jeremy was free to find points of interest on the map. We stopped at a scenic overlook at Decatur, Nebraska. The sun was warm when we got out of the truck, but the overlook was shaded. And in the shade the temperature was much cooler and a hint of the winter to come. The park was on a tall bluff overlooking the Missouri River. From that point we had a bird's-eye view of the endless fields of Iowa. A puff of black smoke appeared above a green corn combine harvesting corn in one of those fields. I'm sure that was a massive and noisy machine, but from where we were it was small and silent.

Autumn colors were still pretty but past their peak. When there was no noise from passing traffic, we could hear the leaves falling around us. We headed north again passing through the Winnebago Indian reservation. When we arrived at the bridge to cross into Sioux City, Jeremy said, "Dad, let's go a little further." The sun had gone down, and the western sky was beautiful. We followed roads along the river to highway 81 and crossed the river into Yankton, South Dakota. We got a room at a small motel and drove back down to Sioux City the next morning. I met briefly with the crew, then drove to the cable company to give them a progress report.

We started toward Omaha again and just south of Sioux City, Jeremy said, "Hey, Dad, pull in here and let's check this out." It was a park called Sergeant Bluff. There was a monument that was a smaller version of the Washington monument. It was the burial site of Sergeant Charles Floyd, the only man to die during the Louis and Clark expedition. He died and was buried here in August 1804. It was a lonely place, even with the busy morning traffic passing by.

Our next landmark along the way was the Sioux City regional airport. Just a few years before, a United Airline from Denver to Chicago, lost hydraulic power, and attempted an emergency landing. One hundred and ninety people died, but one hundred and twenty-five survived the crash. The incident occurred in July 1989.

We rushed back to Omaha after that stop. I had a meeting arranged with a man by the name of Tim Collins. From what he told me on the phone, he was exactly the person I was looking for. He was experienced and he was looking for work. We met at a place called, Whose Pub. Tim had a strong handshake and a friendly smile. His father was black, and his mother was German. They had met and married when Tim's father was stationed there in the army. Tim didn't consider himself to be black or white. He was just Tim. We started work on a large apartment/townhome complex on the south-west side of Omaha. Tim proved to be everything he said he was and more. No matter how hard the work became, he never complained nor lost his sense of humor. If I had other things to do, I could trust him to run things.

Ronnie Barnes and I had rented a section of a warehouse in the industrial district. It had ample warehouse space in back, with an overhead door. The front was glass, with room for a small two-room office. The space had been an automobile radiator repair shop, but it looked as though the place had been vacant for a long time. The floor had a thick coat of dust, the walls and ceiling were covered with a black, oily soot. It would take a lot to make it work, but I knew I could get it done.

The next young man to answer the ad for help, was Shane McNaughton. He was inexperienced, but excited to learn. He referred to himself as an old soul, although born in 1975, he was only twenty years old. Shane would tell anyone who would listen, that he had lived another life and was killed in the Vietnam War. He lived it as a fact and didn't care who failed to believe him. He was a wonderful addition to the workforce. He also asked if there was a position for his wife, Pamela. I told him I would hire her as an admin as soon as I completed the work on the office and warehouse. Pamela said she would do the office work until I was able to hire someone else. Then she would prefer to work in the field with her husband.

There was a convenience store with a deli, near the job site, called Smacks. It was a place where the crew stopped for fuel and home-made sandwiches. My crew and I had come to know the entire staff including the owner, Pat. Tim Collins was running late one very cold morning, when he came flying into the icy, Smacks parking lot, to park in front of the building. He was unable to stop on the ice and he plowed right into the building, caving in the front wall. Everyone inside were shocked. But imagine their surprise when a man wearing a ski mask jumped out of his truck and ran inside. They were sure they were being robbed, but poor Tim only wanted to apologize. He was only wearing the mask because of the cold and he had forgotten to take it off.

There was a young lady working there by the name Jessica Stockwell. I asked her if she would be interested in taking over Pamela's position when the time came, and she said yes. The workforce continued to grow and develop, then US West asked me for an additional twelve workers for home installation. The work in Sioux City was just wrapping up, so I was able to use some of that crew. My son, Jeremy, and Shane McNaughton, were an invaluable force in putting together that project.

Things were running smoothly, but on Friday November 10th, the snow came. It was about eight inches of wet, heavy snow. Jeremy was making a left turn when he got stuck in the oncoming traffic and Tboned. He was not injured, but his truck would be out of commission for some time. He was bitterly ashamed of himself and it took some time to convince him, that it was only the snow, and only an accident.

The snow continued to fall through November and December, and it was extremely cold. Jeremy had become friends with Pamela and Shane, and they were spending a lot of time together. Christmas had passed and I guess he didn't want his old dad to spend New Year's Eve alone. He invited Pamela and Shane to our place for the evening. We had beer, snacks and played a game called Pictionary. It was a fun-filled evening, but the three of them left for another party. Once again, I turned on the TV and watched the ball drop to end the year 1995. Jeremy left for Ohio the next day and again I was alone.

I hired Jessica in January 1996, and Pamela started training her right away. Jessica grew up in Sioux Falls South Dakota. She was from a long line of farmers on both her mother's and father's sides of her family. She said she had ridden on the farm machines with her father and her uncles. Early afternoon they would stop for the day, head for the bar and take her along. They would treat her to pop and candy. When she began to sing along with the jukebox, they realized her talent and started taking her to Karaoke night at the bar. This is where she developed a love for classic country and bluegrass music.

Jessica attended college for a year at South Dakota State University. But she wanted to take a sabbatical. She wanted to travel and search for her dreams in music. Everyone liked Jessica, and she became a good fit in our growing family.

In February 1996, I was invited to Vir-Tech's annual convention in Jacksonville, Florida. It was a week of all-expense paid vacation, except for one full day's meeting at a conference table. Work had slowed down in Omaha, so I said, "Why not?"

On Sunday, February 11th, I got on a plane in Omaha. At about twenty thousand feet the plane popped through the clouds and into the bright sunlight and my entire mood changed. I honestly could not remember a sunny day, since the day Jeremy and I visited the monument at Sergeant Bluff, in November. It was short-lived however, when we started to descend for a connecting flight in Saint Louis it was back to overcast skies.

Jacksonville was sunny, warm and green. It was a waterfront hotel overlooking the beach and the ocean. Vir-Tech had several offices throughout the country and there were people there from each of them. I must have been the last of Vir-Tech's people to arrive. Everyone else was already playing volleyball on the beach. I don't know what they spent for that week of entertainment, but it had to have been a lot. To me, however, it only enforced the notion that I did not want to live in Omaha.

I returned to Omaha a week later to find very few work orders were being assigned to us. I called the phone company and they said things were slow and that was an understatement. There was nothing to do but sit at the office each day and wait. I guess the workers had nothing to do either. So, they waited there with me for a time, then they began to disappear. They could no longer wait, and I couldn't blame them. But it was hard, watching a workforce disappear that I had worked so hard to build. And I knew I would never convince them to return when things became busy again. The phone company had made me a lot of promises that they had not kept. I was losing my integrity and respect for them.

The long days of March dragged on and Pamela and Jessica came to the office faithfully each day and waited with me. Jessica and I were, as they say, 'hanging out' together and drinking beer in the warehouse after business hours. I thought it was because she had nothing better to do. However, we were becoming just a little bit more than friends. After all, we were both adults and neither of us had family in Omaha. I didn't expect anything to come of it, but it was sure nice having someone to talk to.

On a Saturday morning in March, I picked her up and we went looking for entertainment. We stopped at the historic Winter Quarters on the north side of Omaha. It a place where as many as three thousand Mormons built cabins and waited for winter to end before moving on to Salt Lake City. Then we strolled through the nearby Mormon cemetery where hundreds of those people were buried. It happened from 1846 to 1848.

I said to Jess, "Have you ever been to Des Moines?"

She said, "No, I've never been anywhere."

I said, "It's only about a hundred and thirty miles. Want to check out Des Moines?" So, we headed east on interstate 80. Des Moines was a slightly larger city than Omaha and appeared to be exciting for Jessica.

We had lunch and I said, "Want to check out Minneapolis?"

She asked, "How far is it?"

I said, "Two-hundred and sixty miles, straight up interstate 35."

She said, "I've got nothing else to do."

It was after dark when we got to the Twin Cities. Jess had dozed off, I woke her up when the Minneapolis skyline was directly in front of us. Her exact words were, "Wow, no wonder you're bored with Omaha." I was excited to see Mike and the folks at the Lookout. Richard was there as well. We had dinner at the Lookout, then headed south again toward Iowa. She told me she thought Minneapolis would be a fun and exciting place to live.

I thought, *"That's good. Because I might ask you to live there some day."*

Not much happened for the next couple of weeks, except warmer weather. We even had a few sunny days. Winter ended in March, but I didn't breathe easy again until March was gone. Jessica told me again of her

227

dreams of traveling. I had gotten used to calling her Jess. I said, "Jess, you're in the right business if you want to travel." That was April 4th.

Two days after I told her that, I got a call from Jim Sheezer at Vir-Tech's corporate office. He said, "Wynn, you've got that new truck. What would it take to get you to pick up a cable plow machine for us in Baton Rouge Louisiana and take it to our office in Saint Paul?"

I asked, "How soon do you want this done?"

He said, "Yesterday." I asked Jess if she would like to go along and she was excited to say yes.

We left early on Good Friday, April 5th . The route would be interstate 29 to Kansas City, interstate 70 east to Saint Louis, interstate 55 south through Memphis, Jackson, Mississippi, then Baton Rouge. We got to Kansas City and turned east on 70 and saw the signs for both the Kansas City Royals and the Kansas City Chiefs. I guess they shared the same stadium in those days.

We got to Saint Louis and headed south on interstate 55. It was April, but there were few signs of spring, except the sun didn't set until after eight p.m. We stopped for the night at a place called Benton, Missouri. We left early the next morning and crossed the Mississippi River into Memphis, as the sun was rising. From that point and southward, spring was showing. We got to Baton Rouge, and my jaw dropped when I saw the machine I was to deliver. I called Jim Sheezer and told him the machine was much too large to haul with the half-ton pickup I was driving. He was begging, "Please, just try to get it up to Saint Louis and I'll try and get someone from our office there to take it to Saint Paul."

I said, "If I can take it that far, I can take it to Saint Paul."

I rented the heaviest trailer U-Haul had to offer, hooked it to the truck and loaded the machine onto it. Thankfully there was a stretch of four-lane highway leading to the interstate, where I could find out how it would handle on the highway. We hadn't gone a mile when the truck and trailer began to sway from one side of the road to the other. I didn't dare use the brakes to slow down, I took my foot from accelerator and tried to keep it on the road until I was able to stop. In the middle of it all, a young mother with children in a mini-van decided to pass, and somehow, she made it. She was the lucky one, for I had no control whatsoever of what I was driving. When she had passed and all were safe, I said to Jess, "That lady should have to take a driving course about once a month."

It was a tense, white knuckle drive but we made it to Jackson, Mississippi and stopped for the night. By noon the next day, we were passing through Saint Louis. It was Easter Sunday. We stopped again in Iowa and reached the Twin Cities mid-morning on Monday. It was like the city was waking from a long hibernation. The construction traffic that you see little of in winter was plenty. Large trucks pulling trailers with excavating machines and vans with ladders as construction workers hurried to start a short but busy season.

We dropped the machine in the north Saint Paul suburb of Little Canada. We had lunch at a local restaurant and headed south again. But even with my relationship with Jessica, I couldn't make myself feel good about going back to Omaha. I called Jim Sheezer and told him the machine had been delivered. He sounded pleased. He said, "That's great. How's it look for work in Omaha?"

I said, "I have plenty of promises, but right now it's dead."

He said, "You ever hear of Triax cable?"

I said, "I know of Triax, but I've never done any work for them."

He said, "This is an aerial drop rebuild in northern Indiana. Place call Kendallville about thirty miles north of Fort Wayne. Are you interested?"

I said, "Certainly. How soon can we get it under way?"

He said, "We've got people in there now, but we'd like you to run things." I told Jess her pay would be the same if she would like to tag along and help with paperwork. On April 8th, we left Omaha for Kendallville. We followed interstate 80 passing south of Chicago, then through South Bend Indiana. We saw a sign that read 'The Fighting Irish Of Notre Dame'. It's a good slogan, Notre Dame has always been famous for college sports, especially football.

We stopped for the night east of South Bend then drove on in to Kendallville the next morning. We found a great restaurant that would come in handy during our stay. It was called Richard's. Then we discovered Kendallville's number one industry. They manufactured mobile homes. We saw one as we were having breakfast. It was being transported in two sections and two separate trucks and each load was massive. A short while later, two more trucks and two more sections moved west on highway 6, the main east-west route through town.

There were guys there from lots of places, but mostly from western Kentucky. The project was only expected to take about a month. For that reason, it was hard to create a team spirit. Everyone just wanted to do what had to be done and go home. But the weather was perfect, and spring was showing. I remember how fascinated Jess was with all the trees and how tall they were. She had been accustomed to life on the great plains.

The time passed quickly in Kendallville, but one day I needed my driver's license for something, and I didn't have it. Jess and I, as they say, 'wracked our brains' trying to figure out where I might have left it. The last time I could remember having it was when we checked into a motel somewhere in Missouri. I had kept my Ohio license since I was sure I would eventually move back there. I called the department of motor vehicles and they said, "No problem. Just bring in your social security card and we'll issue another." The problem was, that card was in a photo album back in Omaha.

The easiest way to resolve it was to go to the capital of the state where I was born and get a copy of my birth certificate. I asked Jess if she would go along with me to Frankfort, Kentucky. When we returned, I took the birth certificate to the small western Ohio town of Van Wert and got a new license. Before we got back to Kendallville, Jim Sheezer called me and asked if I would pick up another cable plow machine. I was to pick this one up in a little town north of Springfield, Illinois and take it to a repair shop in Fort Wayne for maintenance. Jim told me I would need the machine for an upcoming and long-term contract in Minnesota. It was a large contract for Sprint.

I asked Jess if she was getting tired of all the travel and she said, "Not in the least." We made the trip to Illinois and dropped the machine off in Fort Wayne. On the way out of town, we passed a movie theatre and thought we would stop and see a movie. It was one of the hottest movies of the year. It was about tornadoes in the Midwest. It was called, *Twister*.

Chapter Twenty-Four

On May 7th 1996, we left Kendallville, Indiana for Saint Paul, Minnesota. I called Richard Walter to let him know we were coming. I told him to meet us for a beer. A motel was arranged for us at the Twins Motel in the west Saint Paul neighborhood of Midway. The area and the motel left much to be desired. I had learned that Vir-Tech was not the class act Nacom had been. However, we could make it work until we found a permanent place to live.

It was an old motel that stood beneath a large, age-old oak tree that was just getting green. The motel also stood on a hill overlooking interstate 94, which is an eight-lane highway that runs between Minneapolis and Saint Paul. The noise was horrendous, but the city was alive and exciting. Our room was on the second floor and we had a great view from the outside balcony in three directions. Just on the other side of the highway, the minor league baseball team, The Saint Paul Saints were preparing for a Friday night game at their stadium. Ten miles or so further to the south we could see planes taking off and landing at MSP International airport. We had a view of Minneapolis and Saint Paul from the balcony. There was also a railroad track that ran between the motel and the interstate highway where trains often passed.

Richard was waiting for us when we arrived. I had introduced Jess and Richard when we visited the Lookout two months earlier. They were excited to meet again. The three of us sat on the motel balcony, drank beer and watched the world go by. It was a beautiful spring evening, but it was much cooler than Jess and I were accustomed to, so we called it an early evening. However, before it ended, Richard agreed to work with me.

I looked at some of the work that I was going to be doing for Sprint and knew it would be a successful summer. I also determined that we were going to need some excavating equipment. I called Jim Sheezer and he said that I could pick up the machine I had dropped in Fort Wayne as soon as the mechanics were finished with the repairs.

The Sprint project targeted large apartment complexes. Antenna towers were to be centrally located within each complex. An antenna atop each tower would send and receive signal from a transponder located at the top of the IDS center, the tallest building in Minneapolis. Main cables would be placed underground from the towers to each building where lock-boxes would contain electronics. Crews of installers would place smaller, coax cables to outlets within the apartments. The main underground cables and electronics would be up to me and my crew. Two days later Jess and I were on our way back to Fort Wayne to pick up the needed equipment.

It was a south-easterly journey from the Twin Cities to Fort Wayne. Spring became more apparent as we went, and by the time we got to Madison, Wisconsin, the leaves on the trees were full grown. It was a Friday evening, May 24th. The sun had gone down and lights in the small towns east of Madison were beginning to come on. It was almost dark when we stopped for the night in Janesville, but the robins were still singing. The evening was warm, the lilac trees were in bloom. The upper Midwest air smelled clean and fresh. I was excited about all the work ahead for Sprint. But a haunting feeling came over me. I still had unfinished business in Omaha and US West had already been calling. I wouldn't rule out returning to work in Omaha, but it would take much more than promises.

On the way back to the Twin Cities, we were rear-ended in Chicago. We were on the very busy Kennedy expressway. We were startled, but the guy who hit us sped on past us. He had run into the heavy machine on the trailer behind us. I was sure he hadn't damaged the machine, so I didn't try to catch up to him. We ran into a heavy thunderstorm near Eau Claire, Wisconsin. After that the trip was uneventful.

One week at the Twins Motel was about all we could handle. I rented an apartment on the third floor of an apartment building in the north-west suburb of Champlin. It was called River View apartments and it was located on the south bank of the Mississippi River. Might sound odd, but the river flows east between Champlin and Anoka, angling only slightly to the south. The apartment had everything we were looking for. It was a corner unit on the third floor that faced west and north. From the outside balcony there was a stunning view of the sunset and the river.

There was only one more thing to do before we settled down. We had to return to Omaha to get our things which we had placed into storage before going to Indiana. I called Jeremy and asked him to meet us there, as he had some things there as well. Don Larson from US West called me. He said his boss was visiting from Denver and he said it was very important that I meet with them. I agreed to do so, but I wanted to meet with Brian Blakely. I wanted to know what role Nacom was going to play with US West.

Brian and I met at Goldberg's. The sun was already hot as I walked through the parking lot. Always a gentleman, Brian was seated in the non-smoking section, even though he was a smoker. There was a little small talk, then I said to him, "You know, Brian, it's easy for me to be happy almost anywhere, but Omaha is not my favorite place.

He said, "Tell me about it, Julie and I bought a house down in Millard, but that wouldn't keep me here if Nacom made me an offer elsewhere. But, Nacom's not going to let me go anywhere, with all these promises US West is making."

I said, "Yeah, for that same reason, Vir-Tech's probably going to ask me to keep an office and crew going here."

By the time the conversation was over, my mind was set. I was leaving Nebraska for good and I wished that Brian was going with me. I felt that I was leaving him to a terrible fate. Brian and I shook hands, embraced and said goodbye. I only wish I had known then, that I would never see him again. Brian passed away in 2009. He was forty-five years old.

We settled into the apartment and stocked the cupboard and refrigerator. Minnesota felt like home, even with the long cold winters. In 1996, we had frost on June 4th. Looking back, I had been on the road for more than four years and I was excited to settle down. However, Jess and I had an understanding that our relationship was much like military life. In the event of severe ice storms or hurricanes, I would have to leave for a while.

We both had a spirit for adventure. I asked Jess if she would like to take a weekend adventure to Canada. We left on Friday June 7th. I had been to Thunder Bay, Ontario in 1989, but I was only passing through. It was December 1989, when I set out on an adventure from where I was living in Ohio. I drove north on interstate 75 through Michigan and crossed into Canada at Sault Ste Marie. I followed scenic route 17 north where I stopped for the night in Wawa. Translated from the Chippewa language, Wawa meant wild goose. The folks there are proud of their wild Canadian snow geese. To prove it, there's a wood carving of a massive goose in flight marking the entrance to the town. It had been snowing since I had crossed into Canada, but there was very little traffic and I was in no hurry. However, it was dark when I got to Wawa and I was more than ready to stop for the night.

Snow had covered the ground since October. The snow plows had made their final pass for the night, but the streets were already covered with fresh snow. Christmas lights were hung from the street light poles and every roof, porch and window were decorated. I walked to a little tavern across the street from the motel where I had a beer and tavern pizza. I sat next to a large window watching the snow and the occasional passing of a car. Diane and I had separated earlier that year and I had been living alone. It was in the beginning of what I called, my lonely years. I had been to many places, but this was different. It was harsh, rugged and breath-takingly beautiful. It was cold, but there was no wind and my fascination for the north only became stronger.

The next day, I visited nearby Magpie Falls. I was surprised to see a single black bear attempting to forage one last frozen morsel from a garbage receptacle. It was early afternoon when I stopped for gas at Nipigon. Amethyst is the official gemstone of Ontario and they mine it in the area. They also mine gold and silver in secret locations in the area. In fact, one of the largest deposits of silver ever discovered, was found just to the south, at what is today, Sleeping Giant Provincial Park. Tall, treeless cliffs stand above Nipigon to the north. In town and along the road, northland spruce and birch trees grew, but never getting very tall. The tops of these trees have been torn off by the powerful winds from Lake Superior.

It was dusk when I passed through Thunder Bay and that's when I got my first look at Mount McKay. I stopped for the night in Duluth, Minnesota. Then I drove south to Minneapolis, then turned east on interstate 94 toward home.

Chapter Twenty-Five

Jess and I passed through customs, north of Grand Portage. We were in eastern time and miles became kilometers. We passed a sign along the way that read, 'If you miss Mount McKay, you've missed Thunder Bay'. Mount McKay is the tallest in the Nor'Western mountain range. It stands above the city of Thunder Bay to the south and along the shores of Lake Superior. It had been covered with ice and snow when I was there before. But, on that bright day in June 1996, it was light green with small leaves that had just opened on the birch trees. There were also some small trees or bushes blooming with small white blossoms. I wasn't sure at the time, what they were.

We stopped for lunch at a restaurant at the base of the mountain, where we picked up some pamphlets on things to do in the area. Then we drove up the mountain where the road ended at a parking area about halfway to the top. The view was magnificent, but we were still only halfway. The top of the mountain still towered above us. It looked like a tough climb, but I asked Jess if she would like to try climbing it, and up we went. I suppose it took an hour or so, but we reached the top.

We walked over to the edge of the cliff where we sat down to rest. We could see the truck in the parking lot below and it looked like the tiniest little toy. The city of Thunder Bay also looked like a small toy village, even though it was a city of one hundred thousand. We watched as a large passenger jet slowly descended at the airport below and to the west. We even saw a puff of blue smoke when the plane's tires touched down on the runway. However, we didn't hear the sound of the plane until it was rolling to a stop on the runway. That's when we heard the roar of the engines. I guessed the distance to the airport to have been at least ten miles.

It was obvious that many before us had made the climb. Names, initials and dates were scratched, or carved, into the bare granite of the mountain top. But on that day, there was no one and ours was the only vehicle in the parking lot below. It was a time one wishes could be captured and the day would stay forever bright. Looking out over that city and the endless view of Lake Superior was captivating. The lake is so incredibly blue on sunny days. Jess asked me, "Is there a place to go swimming in that lake?"

I said, "Maybe, but the temperature of that water is just above freezing year-round."

A seagull was floating effortlessly by, on the up-draft, with no fear of falling one thousand feet to the parking area below. Suddenly there was an explosion of white feathers and the poor thing screamed. A bald eagle had darted like a flash from above and snatched the bird in mid-flight and flew away with it. We had just witnessed something one could only hope to see once in a lifetime. We saw the cruel, but indiscriminate hand of nature.

We got settled in and I was happier than I had been in years. I was making lots of money and home every day between five and six p.m. I had been a bachelor long enough to learn how to cook. I made meals for Jess and me, but I also did the dishes, the laundry and the cleaning. It was just a way of maintaining my independence. Anyway, I was happy to have a home-life again. We took long rides on weekends, rented movies and life was good. I guess I wanted something to safeguard against those lonely days in Nebraska. On June 29th, the day after my forty-second birthday we got an eight-week-old kitten from the Humane Society. He was coal black, not a white hair on him. I named him Britches.

Vir-Tech sent in more help for the Sprint project. Among them was a young, good-looking black man, by the name of Jamel Johnson. He was smart-mouthed, arrogant and probably in love with himself. I knew instantly that he and I would be friends for a long time. It's been almost twenty-three years and we're still friends. I had some wonderful and hard-working people that summer, But Jamel and Richard were the key players.

Jess and I returned to Thunder Bay in August 1996. She had taken a job with a medical device company called Medtronic. I thought I would treat her to a weekend getaway before she started her new job. We visited Mount McKay again and that's when I realized what the bushes were that were blooming when we were there in June. What was then white, now looked black from a distance, but getting closer we could see that it was blueberries. Large, delicious and hanging in pods wherever we looked.

From Mount McKay, we drove north to Sleeping Giant Provincial Park, a peninsula that juts about thirty miles into Lake Superior. We saw lots of wild animals in the park, including porcupine, fox and deer. But the highlight was a mother bear and two cubs. The fascinating thing about those animals was that they didn't act wild. They did not shy or run away. They appeared to be in complete harmony with park visitors.

Then we visited Ouimet canyon, also called the Grand Canyon of the north. We made one final stop at Kakabeka Falls west of Thunder Bay. There are lots of rivers, streams and waterfalls north-east of Minnesota and western Ontario. The waters of which appear slightly orange form the taconite, or iron ore, in the region. It was mid-August and there were late summer flowers blooming, but in the north country, it was already autumn.

Through all our travels, Jess was enthralled. However, she told me of places in her home state of South Dakota. So, our next trip was Labor Day weekend, and we visited the Black Hills. We crossed

South Dakota on interstate 90. We drove past vast farmlands in eastern South Dakota where the only thing separating farms were fences. The only trees to be seen are intentionally left to grow along the fence rows creating what farmers call, shelter belts.

The Missouri River flows from north to south near the center of the state at Chamberland. There is a scenic overlook on a bluff looking west over the river. You will not find a more distinct change in landscape from the east side of that river to the west. There are maple, aspen and birch trees growing in Chamberland. But beyond the river, is a treeless, grassy plain. We drove for hours seeing nothing, but it was new to me and there was a stark beauty. We passed an old historic western town that had long since been abandoned. Several western movies had been filmed there, including the Kevin Costner movie, *Dances with Wolves*.

We exited the interstate in Wall. So, named for the white hills of the Badlands located a few miles south of town that stand like a wall above the surrounding plains. Wall is home of the famous Wall Drug. There is a road that runs south passing through a little settlement called Interior. There is a bar there, a laundromat and a few houses, but it's mostly mobile homes. There were barbed wire fences where undernourished cattle nibbled at grass on the hard ground.

The Badlands are a strange place, unchanged for who knows how long. Well, long enough that dinosaur bones have been found there. It looks as though rain had never watered the Badlands. But the washed-out gullies are proof that it does rain there. Along the banks of those gullies, you can see the eons old and multi-colored layers of clay that make up the hills. There are various colors of gray, red, slate-blue, even green. It looks like what one might expect to find on the surface of the moon. And it looked to be out of place.

The sun was setting, and by the time we got back to the interstate, it was dark. When we got to within thirty miles of our destination, we could make out the outline of mountains on the horizon and the lights of Rapid City. It was dark when we checked in, at a Days Inn. I still had the image of treeless plains in my mind. But imagine my surprise when I walked out the next morning and saw the dark green and towering Black Hills. Rapid City lies on the eastern slope of the Black Hills. The view to the west is mountains. The view to the east is the great plains.

There were lots of things to do there. We visited Mount Rushmore, then drove down the mountain into Keystone. Gold was discovered there in the 1870s, by general George Custer and his army. However, the gold rush didn't begin until twenty years later. Keystone was the center of that rush. Some original buildings and relics of the rush are still apparent, and the mountains are still scarred.

Then we drove to Custer, South Dakota, where in 1948, a man by the name of Korczak Ziolkowski, started carving a mountain into a monument. When it is finished, the monument will depict Chief Crazy Horse, atop his horse pointing into the distance. Ziolkowski is long since dead, but the work has been continued by his descendants. The work continues to this day and will probably take decades to complete. When it is finished, an entire mountain will have been transformed into a monument.

There were helicopter tours being flown from a pad near the parking area and we bought tickets. It was near the end of the day and there was no one in line behind us. We were in luck. I asked the pilot where he had learned to fly and he said, "In the Marine Corps." I told him I had been in the corps and we found kinship. We had a lengthy conversation as he continued to fly, he took us close to the face of the monument. Only from there could the scale of the carving be imagined.

It was a lot of curvy, mountain driving to get from Custer to Mount Rushmore. But he lifted us up and over the mountains. Like magic, we were there in a few short minutes. He flew us over and pointed out natural wonders that I was more interested in than anything man-made. He flew us over Harney's Peak and the tallest peak in South Dakota, the 7,064 feet Terry Peak. He flew us low over the Needles Highway. The Needles Highway leads to a natural wonder where granite monoliths surround a crystal-clear lake on a mountain top. Every mountain brought wonder. How and why did it all come about? And how is it that scientists say the

Black Hills are older than the Rocky Mountains, or the Himalayas?

Our next stop was Custer State Park. We saw deer, a coyote and then there were cars stopped in front of us. I had heard of the burros in the park, and there they were checking each car that passed, begging for handouts. If it isn't enough to melt your heart, then there's something dreadfully wrong with you. We all know it's wrong to feed wild animals, but that didn't seem to be a rule at the park. Prospectors abandoned the poor things after the gold rush, and they've been there ever since. They are harmless, lovable creatures. And it's not unusual for a burro to put its head through an open car window far enough to reach food on the other side of the vehicle. Jess had a bag of tortilla chips, and like everyone else, we couldn't resist sharing.

The next time the traffic stopped it was buffalo. There was a large herd crossing the road. They were in no hurry and no one dared to rush them. Signs throughout the park warn of the danger of the buffalo. They were wild and free, but only by the mercy of mankind, for they were once near extinction. So, it's only fitting that they are consigned to this beautiful land.

The narrow road through the park runs along a clear running creek. It's a place where open meadows with golden rod, daisy and black-eyed Susan stand in tall grass. Lying on gentle slopes, the meadows stretch for as much as a thousand feet to the edge of the pine forest. A forest so dark green that it appears black. Hence, the

Black Hills. The forest is where the mountain begins in earnest. If there's a sacred, holy place where one could walk with God, it was here in this peaceful meadow. It's a place you don't feel worthy to look upon. I thought of the words of a Jack London book, 'Mine is but a maggot's life. Nothing more'.

We checked into a motel in Keystone with a magnificent view from the balcony. We could see Mount Rushmore. The motel stood on a hill at the end of town. From our lofty perch, we could watch happy, vacationing people as they scurried from place to place. Every restaurant, gallery and gift shop were packed. Keystone was only a few blocks long and lay between mountains. It was a place that thrived on tourists, and on this last summer holiday bash, every business was making money.

It was a Sunday evening and the streets were noisy until after midnight. The next morning, we sat on the balcony and watched a steady stream of traffic leaving town. Cars with luggage containers strapped to the top. Station wagons packed with all manner of things, including dogs and children. Pickup trucks pulling boats, campers and trailers. We had decided to stay until the next day, which was Tuesday, the day after Labor Day. We thought it might be nice to have free run of the place, perhaps a little more elbow room. The next morning, we had breakfast at the most popular place in town. Except for us and the wait-staff, the place was empty.

I heard one waitress say to another, "Well, it's over now. Another season has come to an end." We walked outside and found the town to be as empty as the restaurant. The streets were deserted and eerily quiet. A melancholy feeling of being left alone came over us. I reckoned it to a child whose school bus had just driven away with his friends and classmates, leaving him all alone. We headed east on interstate 90, and we didn't notice the change until we crossed the Missouri River at Chamberland. The trees and the fields had changed in one long weekend. The corn was brown, the soy beans were yellow and much of the weeds along the freeway were now dead. We left the Friday before, on August 30th, it was now September 3rd. Summer had prematurely and unexpectedly, turned to autumn.

Chapter Twenty-Six

Like all the other projects, the Sprint work ended with the summer. Vir-Tech had no other contracts, so they quietly packed up and left town. I was offered an opportunity to relocate, but I declined. I called my friend, Bruce Rosenfeldt, in Sioux City and asked if he had any upcoming projects. He said he had massive projects, but he was no longer in Sioux City. Bruce had taken a position in Columbus, Mississippi.

Two days later, a Tuesday morning, I walked into the cable company's office in Columbus, Mississippi. The receptionist said Bruce wasn't in and he hadn't worked the day before, but he was sure to be in. It just wasn't like him to miss work. I sat on the tailgate of the truck reading a book for a while, then I noticed an historic marker in front of a house at the end of the alley. I was thrilled when I learned that it was the former home of the playwright Tennessee Williams.

I waited until noon, and when Bruce still didn't answer his phone, I drove to his home. His wife, Karen, answered the door and it was obvious she had been crying. She said Bruce would be OK, but he was recovering at a local hospital. She said, "He was out on Sunday afternoon working on an outage. He was driving his bucket truck when he met a drunk driver on a curve, riding a motorcycle. Bruce swerved to miss him, but the man on the motorcycle was killed. Bruce is going to be all right physically, Wynn, but I don't think he'll be back to work for some time." I wanted to stay and help Bruce, but I needed to work. I headed back to Minnesota.

I took a job with a company called Connectivity Systems Incorporated located in the Minneapolis suburb of Plymouth. It was a union company, so I joined the local 292, electrician's union. I was reunited with a former Nacom worker by the name Tim Traukman. Tim had moved to Minnesota from Helena Montana. He was only nineteen years old when I trained him in the spring of 1993.

We were placing and testing voice and data wiring. It was easy, but extremely boring. I spent entire days sitting in front of patch panels with a testing meter called a pentascaner. It was a beautiful autumn and we were spending it in the basement of office buildings, such as 3M, Honeywell and the Saint Paul Company.

I wanted to make it work, but the first week in October I was asked to travel to Whitewater, Wisconsin, near Milwaukee. It was only a one-week assignment, at the University of Wisconsin, Whitewater. Early October is the prettiest time of the year in the upper Midwest. I drove to Madison and turned east on US highway 12. It had been a chilly morning, but by late morning the sun was warm, and even though the windows were closed, I could smell the autumn.

The project in Whitewater had been ongoing for some time. I was only there to help wrap things up. It was an old, but pretty campus. The garbage cans and dumpsters were filled with beer cans and pizza boxes. Evidence of the previous weekend's college sports celebrations. It's what you could see at any university. Our college kids work hard, but it's impossible not to enjoy their newfound freedom, away from the watchful eye of Mom and Dad.

I was working in a dorm room building. I witnessed something there that I guess I will never forget. It was midday and I was working alone pulling data wires in a long hallway. I thought the building was empty and the students were in class. I heard a whimpering sound somewhere down the hallway and I went to investigate. I found a cute little black girl, sitting on her bed. Her face was in her hands and she was weeping her little heart out. She was obviously old enough to go to college, but she still looked like a little child. She continued to mourn and ask herself unanswerable questions. "How could he? What did I do wrong? What's wrong with me? I just don't want to live any more." I felt helpless. I wanted to call her parents, classmates or someone. Her little heart was breaking, and she needed help. I didn't know what to do. And what still haunts me after all these years, is that I did nothing.

Back in Minnesota, Tim and I were assigned to install a new data system in a school in Waconia, about thirty miles west of the Twin Cities. Waconia was one of the prettiest little villages I had ever seen. It's located on a hill along the south shore of Lake Waconia. The homes are early twentieth century, and post-World War Two style with dormers and screened in porches. Yards and boulevards were adorned with mature oak, maple and birch trees.

The union rules were new to me. Breaks were mandatory, mid-morning, lunch and mid-afternoon. Tim and I took our breaks on the tailgate of our trucks in the parking lot. There was a cemetery on the hill between where we were working and the lake. I was looking out at the brilliant autumn colors and the blue lake beyond. Tim said, "You're not really happy with this job, are you?"

I said, "You know, Tim? I was born to be outdoors. I don't care what the weather is doing, I would rather work outside."

That evening, I read an ad in the newspaper. A small, privately owned installation company was looking for help. I met with the owner and he said he needed someone to do what he called custom hangs. I took the job and custom hangs turned out to be nothing more than work no one else wanted to do. It was service drops that had to be hung to multiple poles or through trees. It was challenging, but it was perfect for me.

It was a short autumn. On November 14th, snow began to fall. On December 28th 1996, the weather man said it had not gone more than seventy-two hours without accumulating snow. We had nearly eight feet on the ground and winter had just begun. The temperature was below normal sometimes as cold as thirty below zero. I never missed a day's work. Jess and I embraced the winter. What more could we do? Once again, I watched the ball drop on New Year's Eve to end the year 1996. But for the first time in eight years, I was not alone.

The spring of 1997 was late in coming, but when it did, it was a little too sudden. There had been record snowfall the winter before and it melted much too fast. We still lived in the apartment building on the south bank of the Mississippi River, and for much of the spring, the parking lot was under water. Further north and west, the Red River of the North was more than thirty-seven feet above flood stage. Cities along its banks were under water, including Fargo and Grand Forks. Fargo bore the brunt of the disaster when a massive fire broke out in the downtown area. Firefighters could do no more than watch, as they were unable to get emergency vehicles in to fight the fire.

I was asked to help with some projects in the Madison, Wisconsin area in March of that year. I called my son, Jeremy, and he agreed to meet me there. There wasn't a hint of spring in Minnesota, but it was spring in southern Wisconsin. Jeremy and I worked together in that area until the beginning of June. He returned to Ohio, and I worked in and around the Twin Cities. Jess and I bought a house in 1997, and I built a getaway cabin for us, about two and a half hours north of the Twin Cities.

We visited the Great Smokey Mountains that year. Jess had always been a country music fan and she was fascinated with everything about Tennessee and Kentucky. We visited Gatlinburg where it was warm and muggy. But when we drove up into the mountains, it was cool, almost cold, in the higher altitude. We drove as far as we could, then hiked to a tower a-top the highest peak in the Smokey Mountains known as Clingman's Dome. We put a coin in a viewing device and supposedly we were able to see into seven states. The view was stunning, but I'm not sure about seven states. Within that view was the smokey haze in the distance that gives the mountains their name.

From there we followed the Blue Ridge parkway to Cherokee, North Carolina, a town on the Cherokee reservation. Route 441 follows the ridge line from Gatlinburg to Cherokee, and is without a doubt, the most scenic in the eastern United States. Mountain streams and waterfalls flow down distant mountainsides like silver chains. Looking Glass Mountain stands like a massive, man-made dome in the distance.

Much of the town of Cherokee is owned and operated by the Cherokee. After the manifest destiny doctrine of the 1830s, Indians were forced to relocate to reservations in Oklahoma. However, some Cherokee hid out in the mountains of western North Carolina. Their descendants now live in Cherokee. It's a much less commercialized town than Gatlinburg. It's much less congested and prices are lower.

Route 19, runs through the town with houses and businesses on each side. A wide and clear running creek flows over moss-covered rocks through the town as well. We found a motel along the bank of that creek, with a full-length covered porch. There were rocking chairs in front of each room where we sat listening to the sound of the water. That night, just after dark, a spectacular thunderstorm came with lightning and a brief downpour. I don't remember the name of the place, but it's easy to find if you ever visit Cherokee.

Summer turned to autumn in 1997, and the weather was much milder. It was as if the earth had blown out all its winter fury the year before. Snow fell a few inches at a time, and it came and went throughout the fall. But it was nothing compared to the year before. We watched the ball drop from our house in Dayton, Minnesota to end the year 1997.

We were back in the south east in 1998, for my son's graduation from bootcamp at Paris Island. It was very late when we checked into a motel in Savanna, Georgia. Jess was just too tired to accompany me to the early morning ceremony. My former wife (Jeremy's mother), her husband and my daughter, Nikki, had driven down from Ohio. They were already seated in the packed bleachers, but I was late. Nikki saw me, left her seat and ran to meet me.

We had given up on finding a seat. I had a new video camera and I was just looking for a vantage point to film the event without blocking anyone's view. Nikki and I were walking behind the bleachers when we were approached by a female master sergeant. She said, "Can I help you, sir?"

I said, "Well I'm former Sergeant Johnson. My son is graduating today, and I'm just trying to find a spot to film it."

She said, "We have a place for you." She led us to the bleachers directly in front of podium.

We were seated among the marine corps' top brass, and top enlisted personnel. The marine corps' commandant does not attend every graduation at Paris Island, but he was there on that day. He was General Charles Krulak, and he was the guest speaker. Jeremy stood in platoon formation very near to the spot where I had stood so many years before. There were probably five hundred in that graduating class. They marched proudly behind the US marine marching band. To be there, with Nikki and my son out on that parade ground, was one of the proudest days of my life.

In December 1998, I was on a crew working in Saint Cloud, Minnesota. It was me, Jamel Johnson, Richard Walter and Greg Moske. We were among a large number of contractors building a communications system for Northern States Power. We were using a directional drill. Directional drills can be used for drilling long distances to install underground pipes or cables. The drill bit can be guided above, below, or around obstacles. We were drilling distances of one block at a time. However, we were having a terrible time directing the drill bit.

Saint Cloud has a nickname, 'The Granite City', and for good reason. Rounded chunks of granite, from softball size, to the size of water melons, lay hidden below the surface. There were several crews and several directional drills, and we were all having trouble directing the drills. As the drill bit went out, it created a hole about six inches in diameter. But then the drill bit was removed, and a device called a back-reamer eighteen inches in diameter was attached. This enabled us to pull back a bundle of pipes eighteen inches in diameter. Cables would be placed into the pipes later.

It was not unusual for a crew to damage another utility, since all the existing utilities ran along the same boulevards where the new system was being added. Power lines and gas lines were damaged almost daily. Most of the new system was placed underground, however, some utility poles had to be added. Everything that was routine changed on December 11th 1998.

A crew working for a contracting company called Cable Construction Incorporated was drilling in an anchor for a utility pole. The anchor, which was to be drilled five feet into the ground, struck granite, deflected and struck a high-pressure gas pipe. It might have been a different outcome today. However, few people had cellular phones back then. When the crew realized they had a problem, they got in their truck and drove till they found a payphone. They called the boss at their office, who called for help.

We were about a block and a half's distance from the blast. I was in my truck and it sounded more like a poof than a sharp bang, but the truck shook. I stepped out of the truck and looked up to see debris high in the sky and still going higher. It didn't take long to realize what had happened. The gas had seeped into buildings through cavities surrounding pipes. It's believed that a furnace, or water heater kicked on, igniting the gas. Four buildings were leveled, four people were killed instantly, and sixteen others were injured. Two of the four who were killed were firemen. Property damage was estimated at four hundred thousand, however, medical and insurance claims would reach three quarters of a billion. Liability insurance for contractors more than doubled after that incident and a law was passed. Whenever an excavator damages an electrical, or power facility, 911 emergency must be notified immediately.

I have never gotten along with safety inspectors on job sites such as the one in Saint Cloud. They're often poorly trained locals who push their authority without knowing what that authority is. The design group for the project was called, Serti, and their headquarters were in Milan, Italy. However, the inspector for our crew was from Brighton, England. His name was John, and for the life of me, I don't remember his last name. I asked Jamel and he couldn't remember either.

I was forty-four then and John was my age, or perhaps a couple of years older. Jamel and I invited him to lunch, and he said to me, "So, Wynn, I heard you were a marine. Ever spend any time on ship?"

I said, "Yes, I did. Did you serve in the Royal Navy, John?"

He said, "Not me, but my father was on the Dorsetshire. They fired the first successful salvo to strike the German battleship Bismarck. He didn't like to speak of it, but my uncles told me about it." John was one of the many, many interesting people I've met along the way.

Excavation halted on the project, but we were allowed to pull cable into pipe that had been placed, and I was allowed to splice in electronics. Some of the work was overhead and I used a bucket truck. I remember days when the high temperature was eleven degrees below zero. It took until midday for the cold to seep through the layers of my clothing. After that, a hot shower was the only way of getting warm.

The remainder of the year was uneventful. The ball dropped to end the year 1998. Jess and I went to south Florida for vacation at the end of January 1999. We stayed at the same Howard Johnson's on Collins Avenue where I had stayed six years before. In the hotel lounge, we found a pamphlet for Dry Tortugas, a national park seventy miles west of Key West in the Gulf of Mexico. There is an old historic military fort on a small island called Fort Jefferson. It was built to protect the Gulf of Mexico from invaders. However, it was transformed into a federal prison in the mid-nineteenth century. It looked like a great place for a picnic.

We drove one hundred and fifty miles to Key West, where we boarded a sea plane with about eight other tourists and the pilot. We were the last to board and we had to sit in the rear of the plane. It was a low altitude flight and the turbulence was terrible. Poor Jess was prone to motion sickness in those days and she became deathly sick on that plane. There was a newspaper in a plastic bag. I stole the bag for her, but even after vomiting in the bag, she was sick until after we had landed.

It was a beautiful place. The fort had been transformed into a military prison in the mid-nineteenth century. The fort covered the island, so I don't remember seeing a beach. However, there was a walkway and we strolled all the way around the fort and Jess was feeling much better. We were touring the open-air cells of the old fort when we came to a sign that read, 'Doctor Samuel Mudd was imprisoned here for more than four years'. You might remember that Mudd was convicted in the plot to assassinate Abraham Lincoln. He was given life in prison for setting the leg of the assassin John Wilkes Booth. For more than four years Mudd maintained his innocence. He was exonerated after he saved dozens from an outbreak of yellow fever.

Chapter Twenty-Seven

Some uneventful years passed, and our traveling was for fun except when Jess had to take an occasional trip for work. In my search for the equipment I needed, we traveled in search of bargains. This took us to Cleveland and Detroit in 1999. We did however, return to Thunder Bay Ontario for a long Fourth of July weekend in the summer of 1999. On the day of the fourth, we were hiking along the Kakabeka River, north-east of Thunder Bay. It was unusually muggy, and the day was hazy. I had never seen that in the north country. I remember saying to Jess, "We'd better start making our way back. Something just doesn't look right."

Through a clearing in the trees, I could see the sky to the south-west was the color of lead. It was about one p.m. when we heard the first rumble of thunder. Within minutes the sound of the approaching storm sounded like bowling balls rolling on lanes. When we got to the truck and started driving, we had a better view of the sky. The clouds were a blueish-black and they were pushing an eerie green in front them. I said to Jess, "This is so unusual. This looks like the storms we have in the south, or central plains." We had a video camera and I asked Jess to start recording the storm. By the time we reached our hotel, rain had begun to fall, and at two p.m., the day was as dark as any moonless night. Our room was on the eighth floor of the Prince Arthur hotel overlooking Lake Superior to the south. We watched the view of the lake disappear like a curtain being pulled from right to left.

Meteorologists said the storm began as a tiny dot near Aberdeen, South Dakota. It quickly blossomed into a massive bow echo, pushing north and east. By the time it reached north-east Minnesota it had become a derecho with eighty mile an hour sustained winds, gusting to over one hundred miles per hour. Roofs were ripped away, and vehicles were overturned. In the Boundary Waters Canoe area more than sixty people were injured, some severely, and tens of millions of trees were knocked down. The storm then turned south passing through the eastern United States to the Gulf of Mexico. The storm then turned north-east and dissipated over the Atlantic Ocean. It is said, the storm had traveled more than eight thousand miles.

We vacationed in New England in the spring of 2000, and Niagara Falls for the long Labor Day weekend. The ball dropped as years passed. I turned fifty on June 28th 2004, and man that was a tough one. That's when the reality of one's mortality sets in. The most a human can hope for, is a hundred years, and at fifty, you're at least halfway through it. At worst, you're near the end. Sure, gives a person a lot to think about.

Richard suffered a bout with prostate cancer in 2001. He lost nearly a hundred pounds and I feared for his life. However, he kept his positive, can-do attitude. He kept saying, "Don't worry, I'm going to beat this thing." And by golly, by the end of 2003, his weight was back to normal and he was his robust self, again. We worked together until late summer 2004. One day he said to me, "You know, mother and I were talking. All our relatives are in Colorado. There's not a thing keeping us in Minnesota. We're going to fix up the house, sell it and move back to Colorado."

For years, Richard had lived with and taken care of his mother, although, she was not the typical senior citizen. Kathryn Walter was completely healthy in body and mind. We spent a lot of time with the two of them and I never saw her falter. In 2003, when she was eighty-seven years old, we invited the two of them to a Minnesota Twins baseball game. She strolled right up the ramps and steps of the Metro Dome like a twenty-year-old.

I noticed that Richard was coughing a lot in the summer of 2004. I said, "Richard, you'd better get that cough checked out."

He said, "Oh, we've got contractors working on the house and the dust is terrible." We said goodbye to them on September 1st 2004. They bought a new house and settled in Greeley, Colorado. I spoke often to Richard on the phone after they moved away. He still had his cough, but what bothered him most was being homesick. He missed his youthful, happy days in Minnesota. But he knew he could never move back. I think he knew he would never see Minnesota again. One year later, he told me cancer had returned to his body, this time in the lungs.

Richard told me of the painful procedures he was undergoing. I spoke with him the first week in April 2006, and he told me that his mother had fallen and broken her hip. I called often during the next few days and there was no answer. We were visiting Jess's folks in South Dakota on Easter Sunday, April 16th. After Easter dinner, I excused myself and walked outside to call Richard. I was elated when he answered. I said, "Richard, before we talk about you, I wanted to ask about your mother."

He said, "Oh... Mother passed away last Wednesday." I called him often after that, but that was the last time I spoke with him. Richard C Walter passed away on Tuesday May 16th 2006.

In September 2004, I was asked to help my long-time friend, Greg Moske, on a project in a little town in Kansas called White City. It was the early days of autumn when I left the Twin Cities for Kansas. Once again, the days were bright, and the foliage was coming into peak colors. I stopped for gas in Owatonna. The sun was warm, but when I walked into the shadow of the building, I felt the chill of autumn and the promise of an early winter. The next time I stopped for gas was in the Missouri hills, north of Kansas City. The sun felt like summer, but the foliage was just as pretty. I felt a nagging regret that I was leaving the autumn colors for the plains of Kansas.

I turned west on interstate 70 in Kansas City in the height of the afternoon rush hour. Downtown Kansas City is located on a hill overlooking the Kansas and Missouri Rivers. Tall buildings on that hill look as if they stretch right into the heavens. I crossed the Kansas River an up the hill leading out of the river valley. As I drove west, for miles I watched in the rear-view mirror, the setting sun glistening on the buildings in downtown Kansas City. There are rolling hills and gullies along the interstate in eastern Kansas. There were tall trees and the colors were still pretty. But the forest ended just west of Topeka.

It was dark when I stopped for the night at the Manhattan exit. I checked into a small motel and it didn't take long for me to fall asleep. The sun was up the next morning when I left the motel, and it was hot. I had driven myself back into a late, but hot summer. I traveled south on scenic route 177 to a sign that said, 'Dwight ten miles' and pointed west. That's when I got a call from Greg Moske. The signal was fading and all I could make out was that Tony was having trouble. I asked Greg where he was and he said, "Minnesota." I knew that Tony Dickie was a young man on Greg's crew, but the call dropped before I could find out where

Tony was. I had Sprint for service, and in those days, Sprint service was good only along main routes. That's because Sprint's owner had purchased a right-of-way from the railroad companies which also shared main routes.

I followed country roads west and south till I finally reached White City. It was a small town and everything about it said farm community. Main Street was at least a hundred feet wide and the only one in town that was paved. Houses closer to the edge of town were one-story white, while those in town were the older style two-story. But they all had porches and patio decks. There were lots of barns and silos, even in town. Grass in the yards was short and only green in the shade of the maple trees. The hot sun had turned everything that wasn't watered, to a light brown. Yards contained swing sets, volleyball nets and barbeque grills. Just like so many small towns, there were all the things folks do for recreation, when there are no other amenities. There was a small grocery store in town with movie posters in the windows advertising the videos they had for rent. There was a bar, a small family restaurant and what had once been a movie theatre. My guess is that it fell victim to the VCR.

I drove west through town and found the phone company's office in a small white building built of cinder block. I was greeted by a receptionist who picked up a phone and said, "Jim. He's here."

Jim was the local manager and he came down the hallway in a haste. He said angrily, "Are you Greg's buddy?"

I said, "I am, what's going on?"

He said, "Man, they've got a mess out there. They cut the main underground power line to a farm and the customer is going ballistic."

I said, "Well, I'm sure I can take care of it."

He said, "Go west out of town, and turn north toward Skiddy. Turn west at the next road and it's the second farm on the right."

The original homestead dwelling had been demolished and a single-story rambler built in its place ten years before. Tall hosta and ferns were planted along the foundation, porch and patio. A large maple tree survived the construction and now shaded most of the house and driveway. To the east of the house, a rusty windmill stood. Symbolic only of a time when windmills pumped water. Beneath the windmill, holly hawk and zinnia grew tall and colorful, thanks only to the garden hose. About an acre of the grounds closest to the house was fenced. Wild parsnip and blue devil plants grew along the fences, dry and wilted in the Kansas sun. A large cattle barn stood to the north of the house, overlooked by pasture land on rolling hills beyond.

I found the two young boys and the farmer. It was Tony and his younger brother. Neither of them looked to be older than their teens. The farmer was perhaps a little older than me. He was a tall man with a sturdy build. He could have stood in a city dressed in a tuxedo and he would still look like a farmer. He had a wide smile and a strong handshake. He said his name was Harmon Gilbertson. He and the two young boys were covered in dirt and sweat.

He said, "Man, am I glad to see you, this ground is like wood." He was helping Greg's crew. Together, they had opened a trench about eighteen inches wide and two feet deep and about twenty feet long, beginning at the house.

I asked, "How do you know if you're digging in the right place?"

He said, "Well, you can see where they plowed in the new phone cable. I just thought we would keep digging along this path until we find where their plow blade cut through the power cable. I remember ten years ago when they trenched in the power cable. They started where we started and ran straight to that power pole by the barn. The main power is overhead from there."

I said, "A trencher is mounted in the center of a machine. Therefore, they would have had to pass to the right or left of the pole."

He said, "Come to think about it, I believe they passed to the left, then trenched over to the pole."

I said, "Then it looks to me like they crossed the power line close to the pole."

He said, "Well I can use the skid loader to open that up."

He went to the barn and came back driving an excavating machine. Within minutes, we found the problem. I didn't even have to tell him what I needed. He said, "I'll run to town, and if Carl doesn't have a splice kit, I'll have to go to Junction City. I told Tony and his brother to fill in the ditch by the house, then they could go. Harmon returned and I had the repair completed and the electricity back on. I was picking up my tools when Harmon, with his wallet in his hand said, "How much do I owe you?"

I was surprised by this and I said, "You don't owe me anything. The question is, how much does Greg owe you?"

He said, "Well I appreciate what you've done. I was in a fix here. I couldn't water or feed my cattle."

We talked for some time, he told me the history of the farm and the generations before him. I said, "You know, there is one thing you can do for me. You could let me go up on that hill in the pasture this evening."

He said, "What for?"

I said, "Just to sit on the tailgate, drink beer, listen to the coyotes."

He said, "You're more than welcome, as long as you don't start a fire. We've been in a drought here for over four years."

I said, "I'll be careful, I don't even smoke."

He asked, "What kind of beer do you drink?"

I said, "Bud Light if they sell it around here."

He said, "They should have it at the bar. They used to have rooms for rent there as well. Might save from driving back and forth to Junction City. My wife has bingo in town tonight. I might just come up on the hill and join you. There's a steel gate next to the barn. You can drive your truck up there."

It was early afternoon when I started my own work. I was accustomed to the moderate temperatures of the upper Midwest, so the day felt miserably hot. By about three p.m. a line of gray clouds formed in the sky to the south-west. Each time I looked in that direction the clouds appeared to have grown heavier and moved closer. I kept thinking how refreshing a cooling shower would be.

It was about six p.m. when I walked into the bar and asked about the room. I seemed to remember the bartender's name was Lisa. She laid down the basic rules. "No smoking, no pets and no getting drunk and breaking things. That'll be forty-five dollars plus tax." I asked about food and she said, "We sell tavern pizza till ten p.m. After that you're on your own." There were steps on the west end of the building leading to the rooms above the bar. The room smelled musty, but it looked clean and it had a large window overlooking the street. I turned back the covers to check for spiders and scorpions and found nothing.

I took a shower, got dressed, bought some beer at the bar and headed back out to the farm. The clouds hadn't moved much in the hour or so since the last time

I noticed, but they were still there. There was a great view from the hill. I was looking down on the roof of the house and barns. Beyond the house I could see the white dust that had formed on the shabby trees and weeds on each side of the road. The slope ran upward to the east and north. I couldn't see the house, but I could see the barns and silos of the neighboring farm a quarter of a mile or so to the east. There was a cornfield to the west, and beyond the road to the south, a soy bean field. The pasture had been trampled and the grass nibbled clean, except for some blue devils, milk weed and wild parsnip. It was as if the cows had been careful not to step on those plants. As if they had set them aside for a specific purpose, or just to look upon.

The day was still hot, but the cold beer helped to cool me down considerably. I heard a crunch in the dry grass and Harmon said, "Well, how'd the rest of your day go?"

I said, "Fine, except it was so damned hot."

He said, "You should have been here in July and August."

I said, "I been watching that cloud. Maybe we'll get some rain."

He said, "No, don't pay any attention to that. You'll see that a lot, but it never amounts to anything."

Harmon was enthralled when I told him of my life on the road. He said his forefathers had come to Kansas as part of the Homestead Act. But then he had an interesting story to tell as well. Harmon Gilbertson had the best argument for reincarnation I had ever heard. He didn't tell the story as if he were trying to convince me to believe him, he spoke as if he had recently moved from his previous life. He spoke of having been a mason worker. He told lucid stories of living in a great city but living with his wife and child in a small house in a suburb. He wasn't sure where the city was, but he remembered seeing the sunrise over the water. He said, "Could've been Chicago, could've been Boston, could've been somewhere overseas."

He was like Shane McNaughton of Omaha. He told his stories from the standpoint of someone who had to have been there. He spoke of weights, measures and the specialty tools he used in masonry. Then he spoke of how he died to end his previous life. He said he had sat on the edge of a building with a co-worker having lunch as they did each day. He said they enjoyed the fresh air and the lofty view of the city below. But when the break had ended, he placed his hands on the bricks to push himself up. However, the bricks gave way and he fell to his death. I wish I could remember the detail in which he told this story, but it was enough to convince me that he had lived another life.

Shortly after he told his story, we saw a car coming from the east in front of a cloud of dust. It slowed then turned into the driveway.

He said, "Well, my wife is home. She brings pizza on Monday nights. You're welcome to join us."

I said, "No thank you, Harmon, think I'll sit here for a few minutes then head to town. I really enjoyed this. Is it OK if I come back tomorrow?"

He said, "Come as often as you like, just remember to close the gate behind you."

It was dusk when I heard the first yelp of a coyote, they never seem to make the same sound twice. They were somewhere in the distance, and with all the animals safe in the barn, they would probably keep their distance. But a farm is never completely silent. If not for the stillness of the evening the sounds would go unnoticed. Cattle low or find something to clunk in the barn and the windmill squeaks. Night began to erase the silhouette of the farm to the east. To the west, what I thought would be rain clouds were thin enough that I could see a quarter moon just above the horizon. It was time to call it a night.

I worked in and around White City through the bright, but not so hot, days of October. I returned once again to the hill for a last look and to say goodbye to the Gilbertson family. The leaves of the maple tree covered the yard and crunched under my feet as I walked to the front door. Harmon was in the field harvesting. I spoke briefly with his wife, then drove up the hill. The sun was setting much earlier and the greens of summer were gone. The fields were brown and the few leaves that were left on the shabby trees along the road were brown. Once again, I had seen the rapid change from summer to autumn and it was time for me to leave.

Chapter Twenty-Eight

Once again, we watched the ball drop to end the year 2004. Hurricane Wilma hit Miami on October 27th 2005, and I found myself back in south Florida, the first week in November. There was a crew of thirty-two of us, and except for Jamel and me, they were from Canada. I was given the address for a Days Inn hotel on Collins Avenue. It had been thirteen years, but I thought it must have been close to where I had stayed before. Imagine my surprise when I found that Howard Johnson had sold to Days Inn. It was the same hotel, the same everything, just a different name.

The hurricane had been the most powerful in history. But thankfully it weakened to a category three before it made landfall in south Florida. However, this is not to downplay the devastation. The damage was estimated at twenty-seven billion dollars. The path of the storm was further north than Andrew had been. Areas affected were Miami Springs, Opa Locka, Hialeah and north Biscayne Bay. The work was being done once again for Bell South, and the nature of the task was the same. We were very well paid, but we were obligated to ten hours and day seven days per week. We were given every other Sunday off to do laundry and other personal chores. My son, Jeremy, came down from Ohio and it was fun working with him. Jess came down and visited for a week during Christmas. She was gone before New Year's Eve. Like thirteen years before, I sat on the bed alone in my hotel room and watched the ball drop to end the year 2005.

I worked until the end of February 2006 and returned to Minnesota. Jess had to go to Seattle for work in August 2006, and I tagged along. We went to Mount Saint Helens, Mount Rainier and to the top of the space needle. However, the highlight of the trip was whale watching off the cost of Washington. We spent five hours at sea, and we were both cold and wet when we got back to the resort town of Anacortes. The day had been cool and overcast, but the afternoon was warm and sunny. I was home with Jess when the ball dropped to end the year 2006.

In the spring of 2007, I worked till the end of May in Brookings, South Dakota. Then I worked for about six weeks on the northern plains of Minnesota, north of the upper and lower Red Lakes. I was there for the summer solstice and I remember that I could still see twilight in the sky well after eleven p.m. That project done, I headed to the little oil well town of Russell, Kansas. I went from the cool damp of the Northern Plains, to the stifling heat of July, in the Central Plains.

On December 8th 2007, a crippling ice storm hit northern Oklahoma. I spent a month replacing downed overhead lines for AT&T on the north side of Tulsa. I watched the New Year's Eve ball drop alone in my motel in Broken Arrow, Oklahoma to end the year 2007. From Tulsa I went north to the little town of Bentley, north-west of Wichita where I did aerial splicing and line maintenance for United Telephone.

The I went to Baxter Springs, Kansas for a sizeable underground project. I was in Baxter Springs long enough to develop a routine. I worked alone and I worked six days a week. I went to the laundromat on Sunday mornings. Then I would drive twenty-five miles east to Walmart in Joplin, Missouri for groceries. On May 22nd 2011, an EF-5 tornado hit the town of Joplin. One hundred and fifty-eight people were killed, and more than a thousand wounded. Joplin was devastated including the Walmart.

Baxter Springs and nearby Pitcher, Oklahoma, were built as a result of lead mining. It is said that two city buses could be parked side by side and end to end in the underground lead mine, stretching from Baxter Springs to Joplin. With the discovery of lead poisoning, officials were making every attempt to clear everyone out of Pitcher, Oklahoma. It was almost deserted when I was there, but three months after I left, nature dealt the final blow. On May 17th 2008, a tornado destroyed what was left of Pitcher.

I finished the job in Baxter Springs on the third week in February and went home to Minnesota, but not for long. I needed another cable plow for upcoming projects in Minnesota. Jess, who is the queen of search, found one in Portland, Oregon. On Friday February 22nd, Jess and I flew to Denver, to Los Angeles, and to Portland. I bought the cable plow and loaded it onto a rented truck, and we started the nearly eighteen-hundred-mile journey home.

We were just leaving Portland when my phone rang. It was my sister, Lily. She called to tell me that our mother was dying. Doctors were saying it could be hours, or it could be a week, but her death was inevitable. Her health had been failing for some time, but this was the absolute worst time. I couldn't just park the truck somewhere and go. Frankly, I wasn't sure what to do.

We drove east on interstate 84 along the south side of the Columbia River gorge. My plan was to work my way north and east into eastern Washington where I would turn east on interstate 90. I would follow 90 to Billings, Montana, then on to Interstate 94 which would lead us back to the Twin Cities.

We turned north on interstate 82, then got on highway 395 at Kennewick. My plan was to stop for the night at a little place called Ritzville. It was late February and the land in eastern Washington was brown, treeless and secluded. It was a long stretch of two-lane highway from Kennewick to Ritzville and I was sure I didn't have cell phone signal. Jess fell asleep and that gave me even more time to think. It gave me time to wonder if my mother was still living. Then I would have to remind myself of what I was being forced to think. Is my mother dead?

I could see my mother and I could hear her voice so vividly. But I couldn't imagine her on her deathbed. She was such a fascinating person. She outlived my father by almost twenty-five years, and she lived alone after his death. But she told me on more than one occasion, that she was not lonely living alone. Besides me, she had close friends and family close by when she wanted company. And she had her animals. She had that noisy little mutt she called Sadie, and a talking bird named Sherman.

Experts will tell you that a talking bird is only mimicking the sounds they hear. But I'm telling you, Sherman would hold a two-way conversation with you. For instance, he would ask for a cookie and if you told him no, his response was quite colorful to say the least. Then my mother would become enraged and say, "Somebody ought to wring his neck. I won't allow such language in my house." But it was hard to be angry with the bird when every word he spoke was in the sound of her voice.

Sherman would ring like the phone then say, "Don't answer it." He barked like the dog, growl like the dog then join my mother in her snoring. People would come to visit, and they would look around for a vicious dog. But my mother would say, "Don't worry. It's only Sherman. Sherman, honey stop growling."

He had seen people stand in the doorway twirling keys saying, "I'm leaving."

Hence, his favorite toy was a set of keys on a ring. He would stand on one foot, twirl his keys and say, "I'm leaving."

Sherman didn't live in a cage, he only slept in one. During the day, he walked about the house talking to himself. At night he was told, "Sherman! Go home." He would obediently climb into his cage at which time a cover was placed over the cage and he would become quiet.

Then he would call out in a loud voice, "Gooood night." And there would not be another sound from him until morning.

My hope was that I would make it back in time to get to Kentucky before her death. We made it to Ritzville where we stopped for the night. We got under way early the next morning and stopped for lunch in Spokane. After that snow was falling throughout much of the day and it was mountain driving. I thought about my mother a lot that day. It was February 24th, and it was her birthday. We crossed the Chimney of Idaho and the snow was falling faster. I had hoped to make it to Billings, but the road was getting slick.

At dusk, Jess fell asleep again and I thought it was for the better. No sense in both of us being nervous. But this gave me more time to think. My mother loved the farm life and she loved having farm animals especially chickens, maybe even a pig or two. But it was hard to have farm animals when the edge of her yard was the edge of the wilderness where countless predators roamed the night. She used to say, "If I only had a barn."

One day, my brother, Jimmy, walked up and sat down beside her in the porch swing. He said to her, "Charles and me, we're going to build you a barn."

She was overjoyed at first and then she said, "Wait a minute, Jimmy. You're either drinking or lying, one or the other."

He said, "No! we're going to build you a barn." And build a barn they did. It was perfect in every way. It was built of rough sawn oak lumber straight from the forest nearby. It had a long-lasting metal roof and a covered porch enclosed with wire fencing. Her animals had the safety of the barn and a place to enjoy the outdoors. And they built it just about thirty feet from her own porch. She spent hours in her porch swing admiring her barn and watching her animals.

She once said to me, "It's not having what you want, it's wanting what you have, and I've got just about everything I could hope for." And I must admit, she had a lot. She had shelves and curio cabinets filled with whatnots and knick-knacks. Every item with its own story to tell. "This one came from your grandmother and that one was given to me by Hazel Vanover. You remember the Vanover's don't you?" It was her way of never forgetting her friends and loved ones. And it seems to me that she valued the most worthless items even more. She even kept the letters I wrote from overseas.

Her yard was filled with flowers and fruit trees. All of which were carefully looked after by her children who lived close by. Our youngest brother lived just across the creek from her, and she ruled him like an iron boss, while he humbly obeyed like a good shepard.

Long before the days of social media, she had her own social network, in the form of a CB radio home base unit. She was on the air till the wee hours of the morning with listeners as far as fifty miles away. Sometimes she talked, sometimes she played records and sometimes Sherman would entertain listeners. Oh yes. Everyone loved Sherman. He was invited to speak on a real radio station in Whitesburg. My sister, Rose, took Sherman to the station and even though Sherman hated Rose, he was a hit.

We all must face death and we would all prefer to die in our sleep. But that doesn't always happen, and my mother had the agony of knowing that she was dying. She had been at the King's Daughter hospital in Ashland for a few days and the medical staff were not saying much of anything of her condition. A doctor paid her a visit, and my brother, Charles, was waiting in the hall when he came out of her room. Charles said to the doctor, "Can you tell me what's going on with our mother?"

The doctor said, "What's going on is, your mother is dying. Her kidneys have already shut down and her system is being poisoned. When that poison reaches her heart, she's dead. I'll sign her out if you want to take her home to die. It could take hours, or it could take a week, but there's nothing that can save her. And someone's got to tell her."

With that, the doctor walked away. Charles took a deep breath. He had to come up with a way of telling our mother. He sat down in a chair next to her bed and said, "I'm afraid I have bad news."

She said, "What? Are they not going to let me go and be home for my birthday?"

Charles said, "No, it's worse than that. He says you're not going to make it this time."

She said, "OK, I would prefer to die at home."

We stopped for the night in Rocker, Montana. My phone rang just after midnight. It was my sister-in-law, Bonnie, calling with the news that my mother was gone. She died one hour after her eighty-fourth birthday ended. She had requested a short funeral service. My brother, Charles, was the executor of her estate. He said he would postpone the funeral to give me time to get there, but I told him to carry out her last wishes.

When I got home, I booked a flight to Lexington, Kentucky. I didn't make it in time for the funeral, but I spent almost two weeks with my family. I headed home to Minnesota with the notion that it would be time to start the season by the time I got there. I boarded a plane in Chicago on a connecting flight. My hopes of starting an early season were dashed, when the pilot spoke, "Ladies and gentlemen, we will be landing in Minneapolis/Saint Paul at nine twenty a.m., where the temperature is seven below zero."

In December 2008, I was back in Oklahoma. Windstream Telephone was upgrading their underground service cables to homes. Once again, I settled into a motel in Broken Arrow, south-east of Tulsa. I worked in eastern Oklahoma for about three weeks, then headed south-west, and settled into a motel in Ardmore, Oklahoma. It was there that I watched the ball drop to end the year 2008.

Jess and I watched the ball drop together to end the year 2009. On December 3rd 2010, I took a crew to Laddonia, Missouri for a lengthy underground project. Laddonia was north-east of Mexico, Missouri. Mexico became famous for manufacturing clay tiles for the space shuttles. The only things Laddonia could boast were a Casey's gas station and The Hard Ride Saloon. We worked through December, but we had to place the project on hold through the month of January due to snow and frozen ground. We headed out to the west Texas town of Odessa. It was there in a motel that I said goodnight to Jess on the phone, and watched the ball drop to end the year 2010.

Three weeks in Odessa, then we traveled five hundred miles east to Corpus Christi. We were there for about three weeks when I got a call from the phone company in Laddonia. The weather was better in Missouri and we were told we could finish the project. We returned to Laddonia in late February. What I remember most about the final phase of that project was going to Martinsburg to pick supplies from the phone company. It was about twenty-five miles during heavy thunderstorms. I remember being chased like a rabbit in front of a tornado. I would turn one way and the twister would appear in front of me. Scary times, but I got out OK.

On March 22nd 2011, I called my sister, Lily, to wish her a happy birthday. It was spring, the grass was green, and the birds were singing. She told me her daughter, Angel, was awfully sick. Then she said, "Well you've been on the road for almost four months this time. When are you going home?"

I said, "Today, Lily. I'm going home today."

End Notes

The daughter my sister spoke of, passed away later that year and I wrote my first book about her. My brother's wife, Bonnie, who called with the news that my mother had passed, died suddenly of a heart attack in May 2015. As we get older, we see our friends and family members fade away. I finished this manuscript on February 10th 2019. And in the early morning hours of that day, my brother passed away. There is no measure for the emotions. After the shock and the sorrow, comes the pointless anger. You want to blame someone. The medical staff, or even the victim. Secretly you say, *"He just didn't take care of himself, or the doctors didn't know what they were doing."*

Then you make some arrogant promises to yourself. You're going to eat right, exercise, lose weight, live to be a hundred and die in a mountain climbing accident. I too, had these notions. I thought I was healthy in every way until I was diagnosed with degenerative disease of the spine in 2015. Nature uses one ailment to create others until one day we lose all hope. I used to love to run and now it's painful just to walk. But, my doctor says, "Keep moving." Therefore,

I will continue to work. But that's OK, I've always loved to work.

When I was very young, I had dreams of travel, but I did not expect it to become an addiction. However, I was fortunate to have made a good and honest living along the way. In early December 2016, Greg Moske and I traveled to the south-west Kansas town of Cimarron, fifteen miles west of the old west town of Dodge City. We spent almost three months there working for United Telephone installing fiber optic cables.

I had a hard time accepting my mother's passing, but she's been gone for almost eleven years now. As our loved ones pass, they pave the way for our own demise and none of us are exempt. But I think it makes it easier for us to accept our own impending fate, to say, "If he, or she did it, then I can do it." Richard Walter was my greatest inspiration for this. He died with such dignity. He didn't embrace death, but he accepted his faith so bravely.

Jess still works in the medical device industry. She travels to lots of places for work and often to Miami, Florida, or Portland, Oregon. I sometimes tag along for fun. I still travel often for work or to a book event. I have never taken my life for granted. I have tried to enjoy as much of it as possible. Perhaps that's why it has passed so quickly. But I love to travel and the Sojourn Life continues… for now.

CPSIA information can be obtained
at www.ICGtesting.com
Printed in the USA
LVHW020855300322
714730LV00005B/117

9 781800 163270